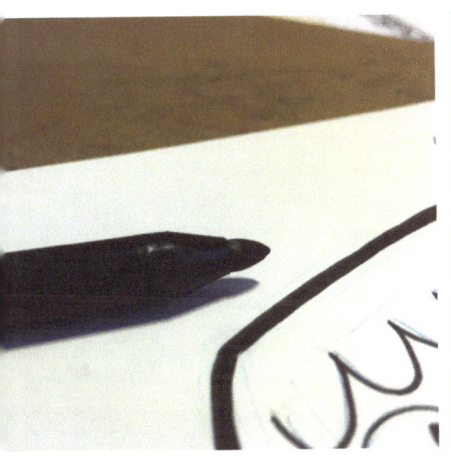
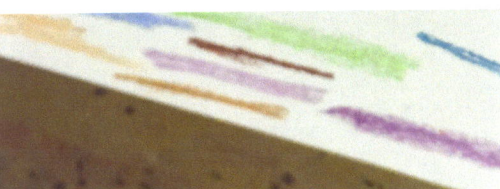

VOLUME TWO

I0511281

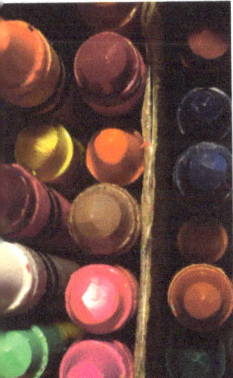
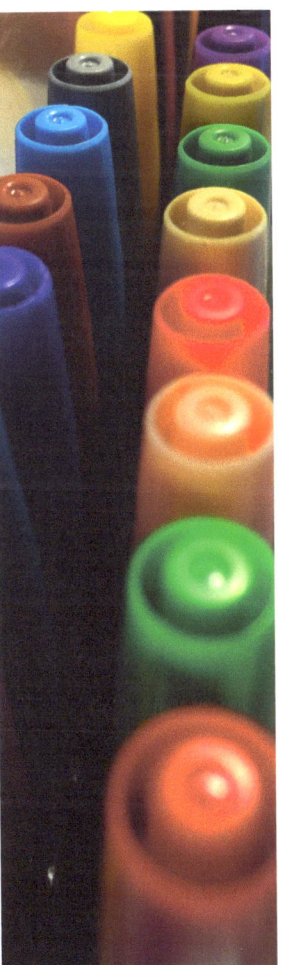

ART BY MARK

Mark Mariano

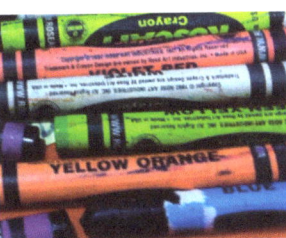

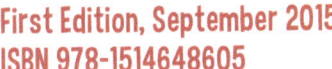

First Edition, September 2015
ISBN 978-1514648605

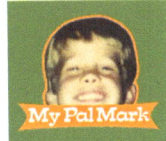

My Pal Mark

ART BY MARK VOLUME TWO. Published by My Pal Mark. My Pal Mark is a trademark of Mark Mariano. All the art in this book is from 2010-2014 and was created in parody using pencil, markers, ink, and crayon. Mark claims no copyright to the characters that aren't his. All characters appearing in this book are Trademark and Copyright by their respective creators/owners. Find Mark's original books at MyPalMark.com

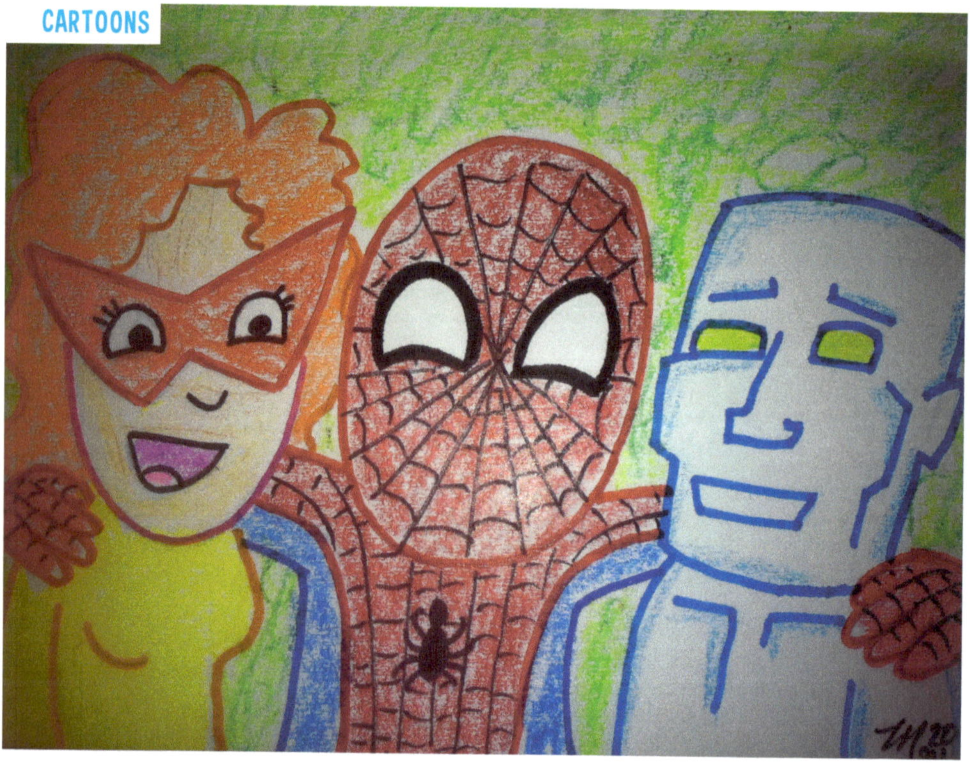

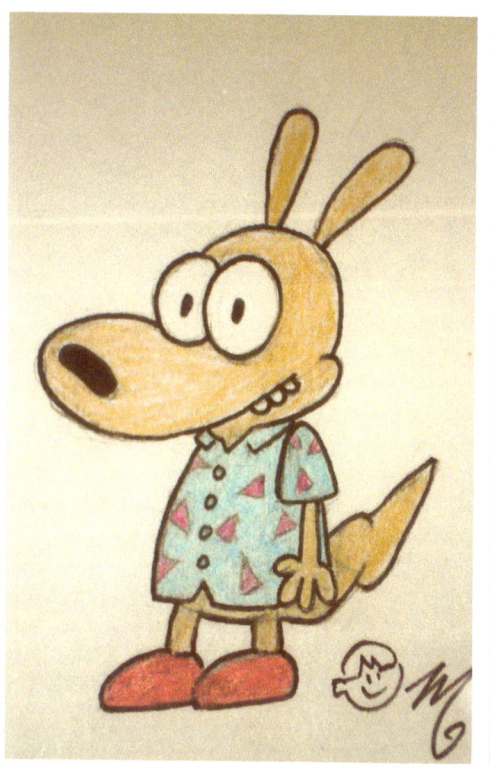

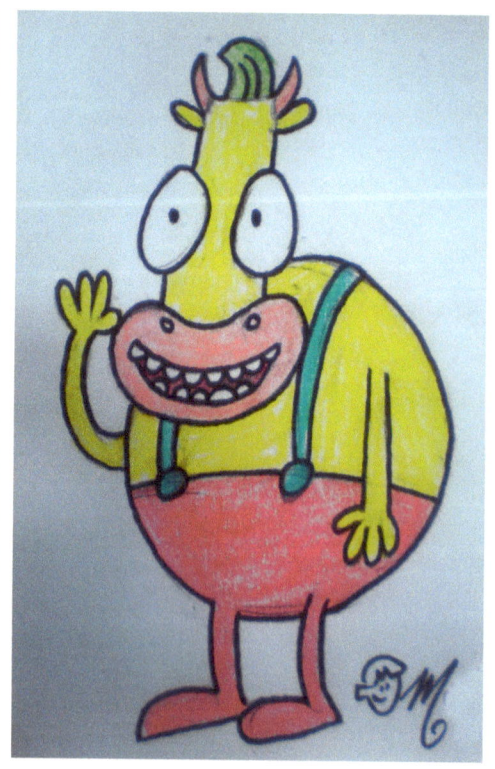

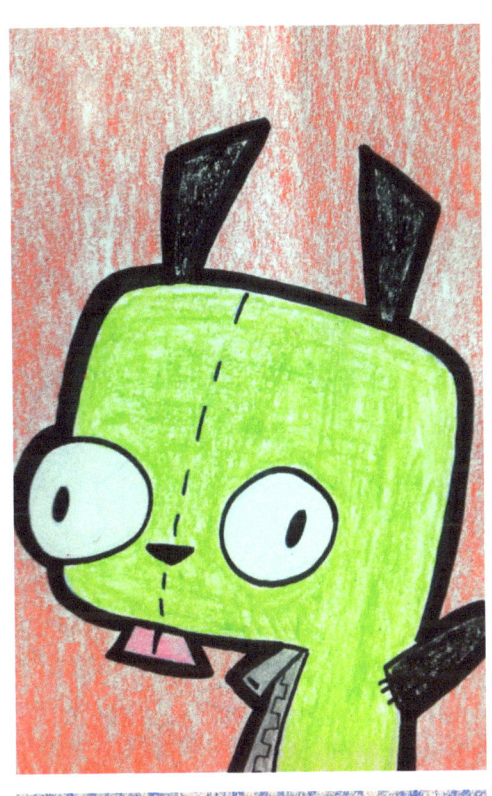

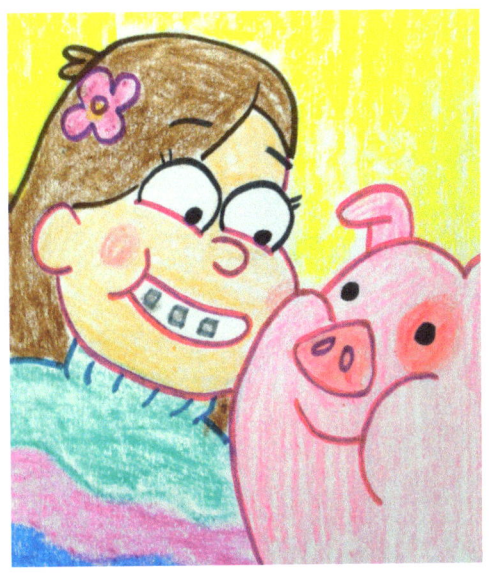

OTHER PAGE: Spider-Man and His Amazing Friends, Rocko, Heffer
THIS PAGE: Gir, Mabel and Waddles, Pink Panther, Beetlejuice

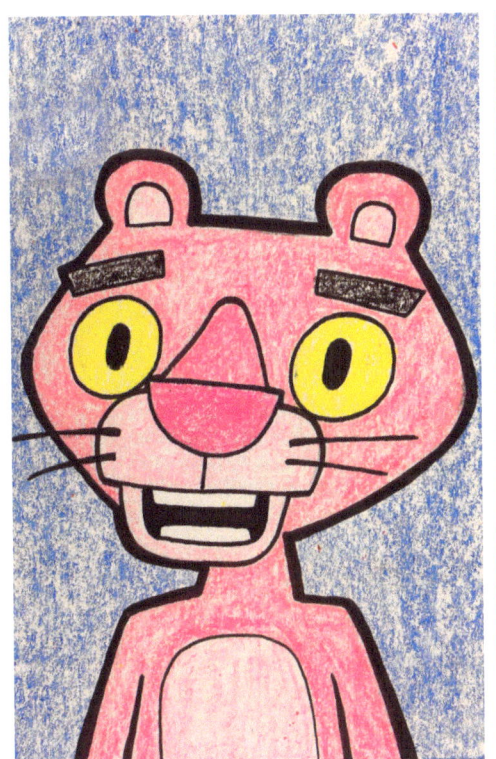

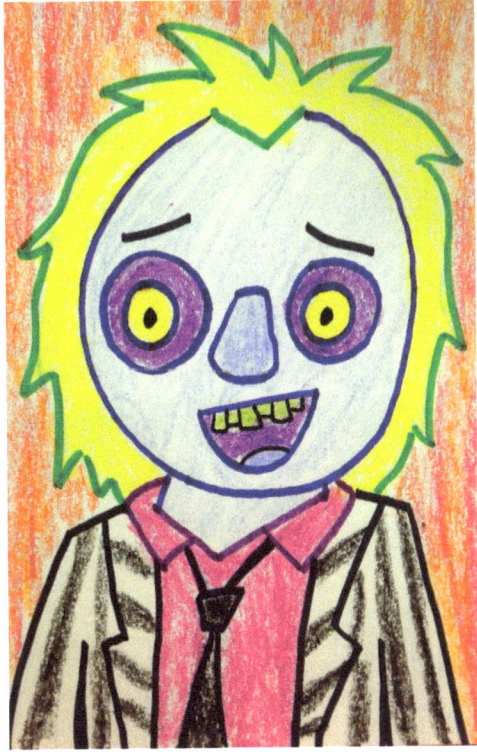

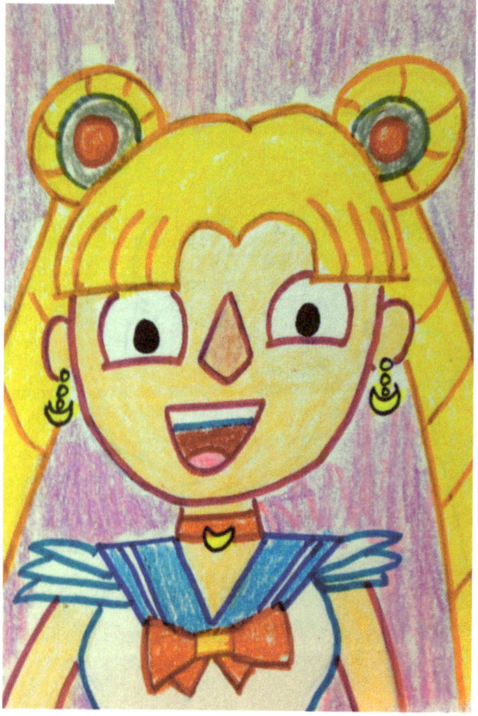

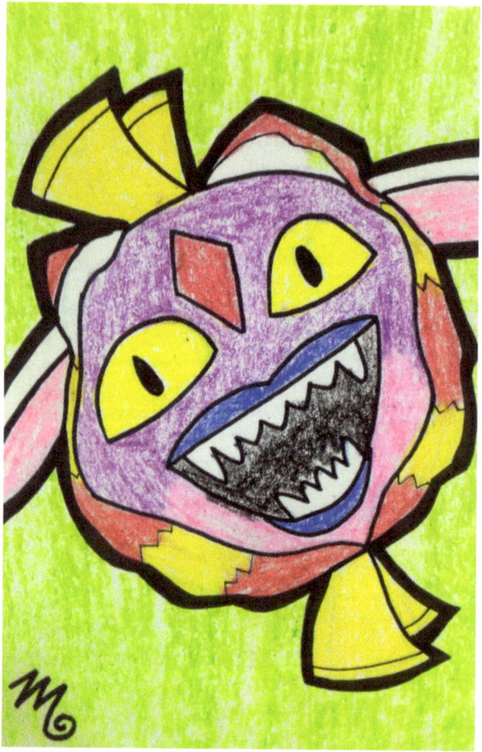

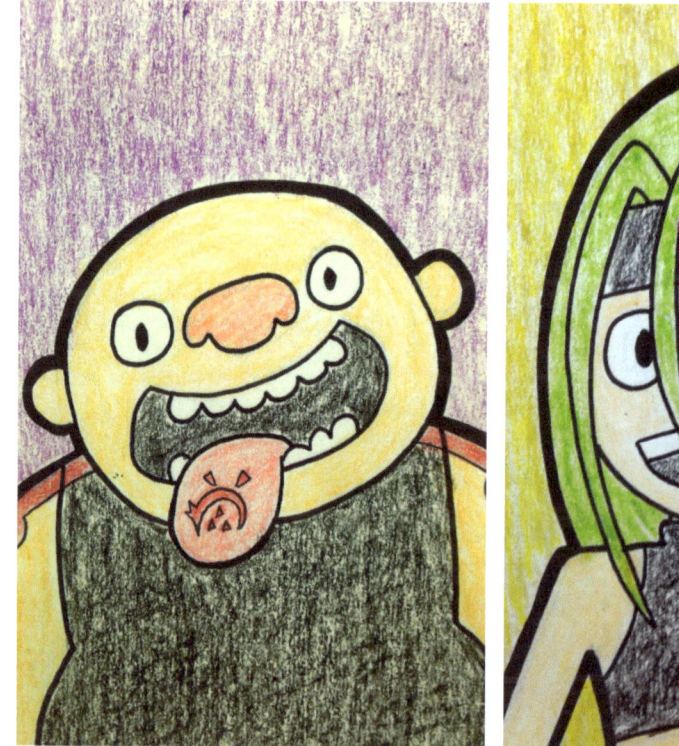
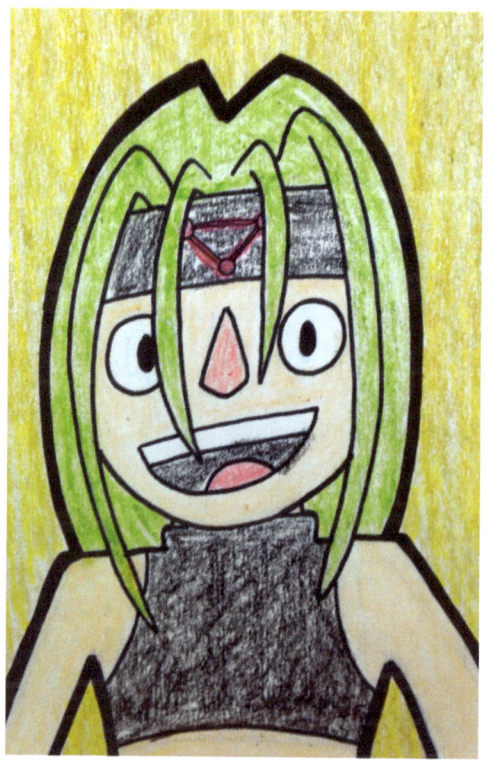

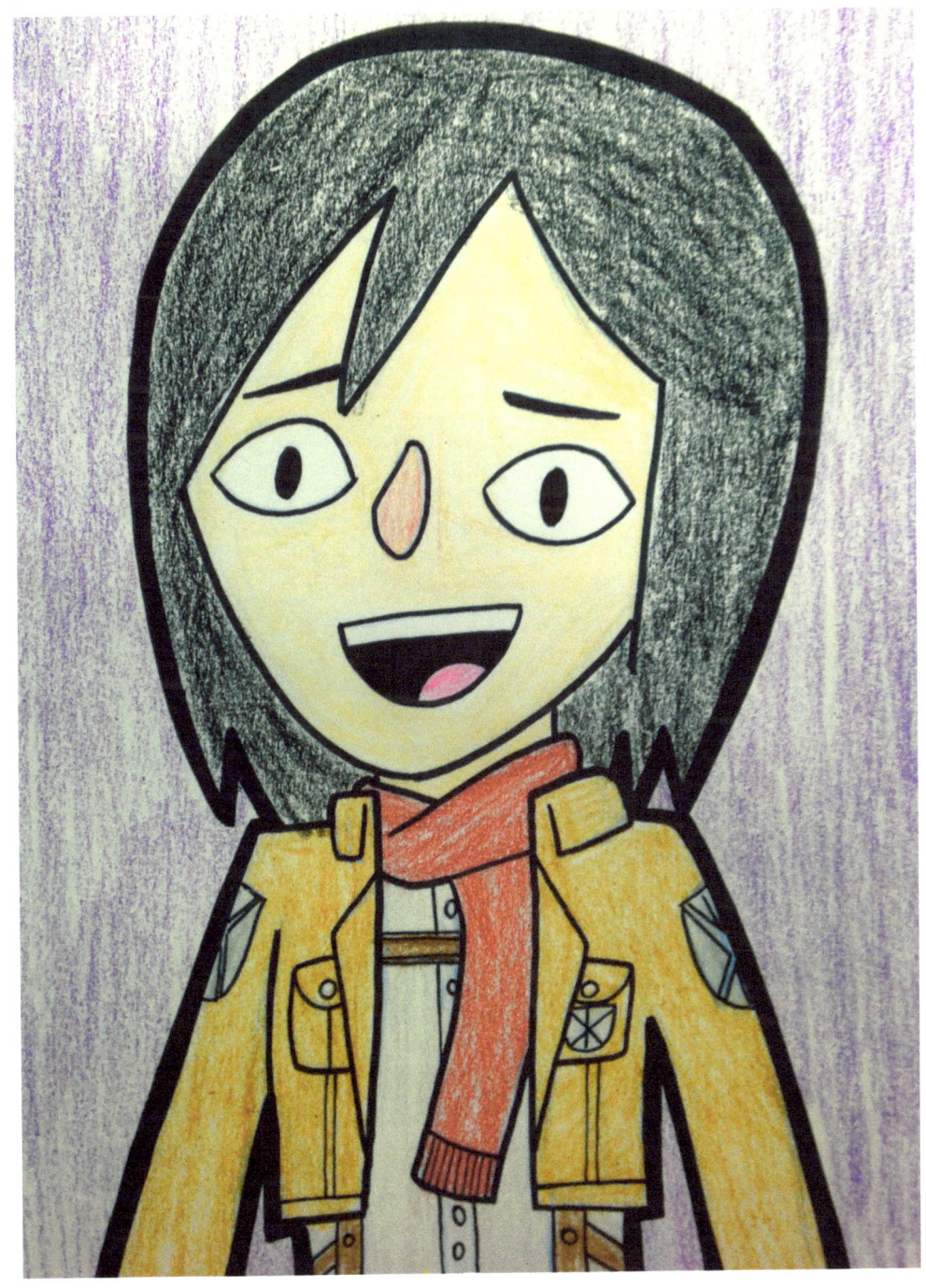

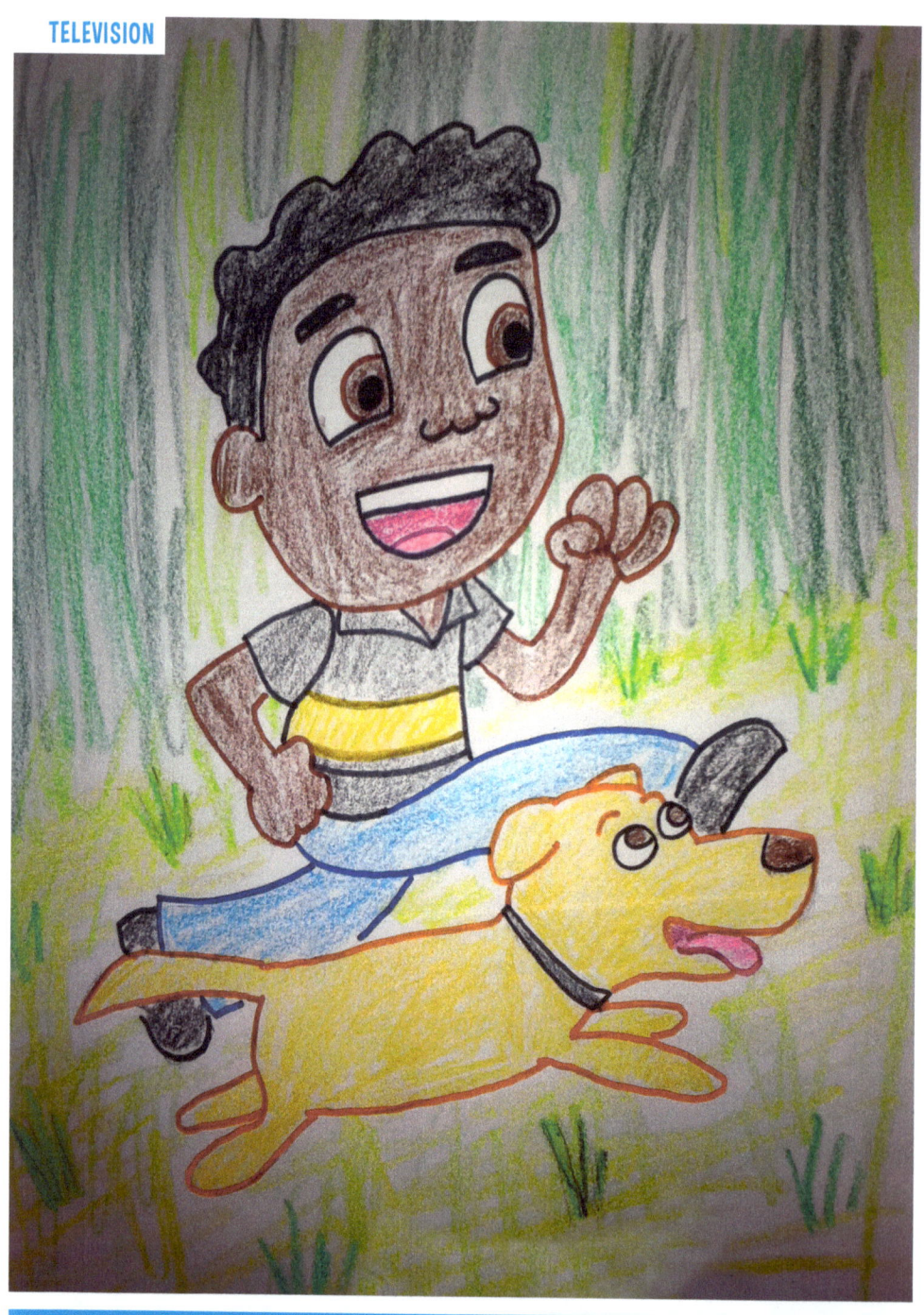

THIS PAGE: Walt and Vincent

OTHER PAGE: Ron Swanson, Sleestak, Castiel, Buffy, B.A. Baracus

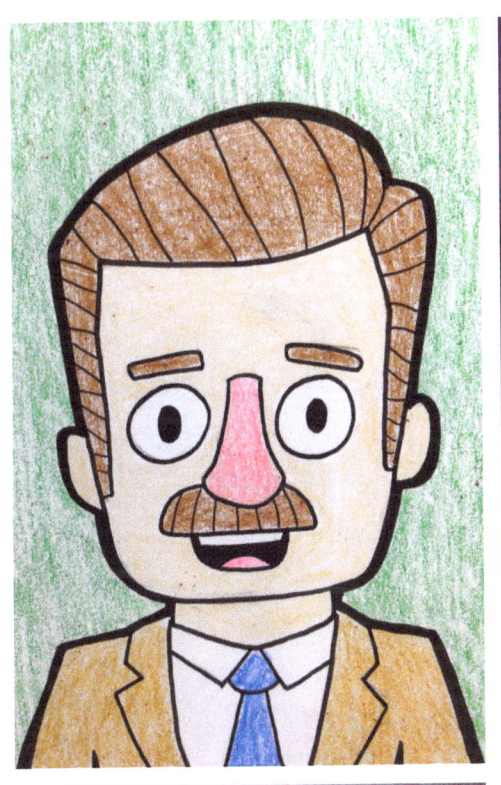
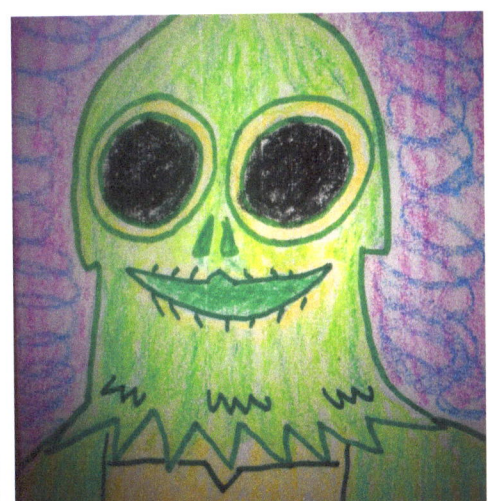
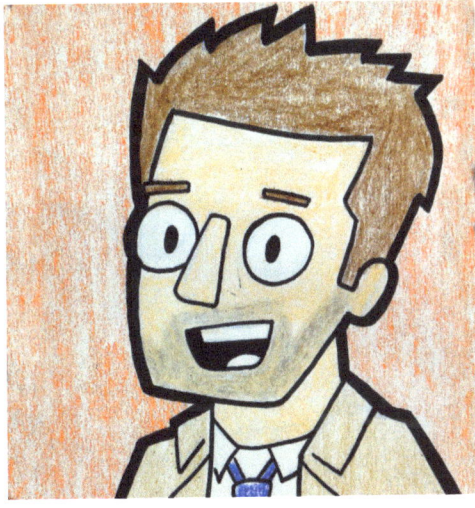
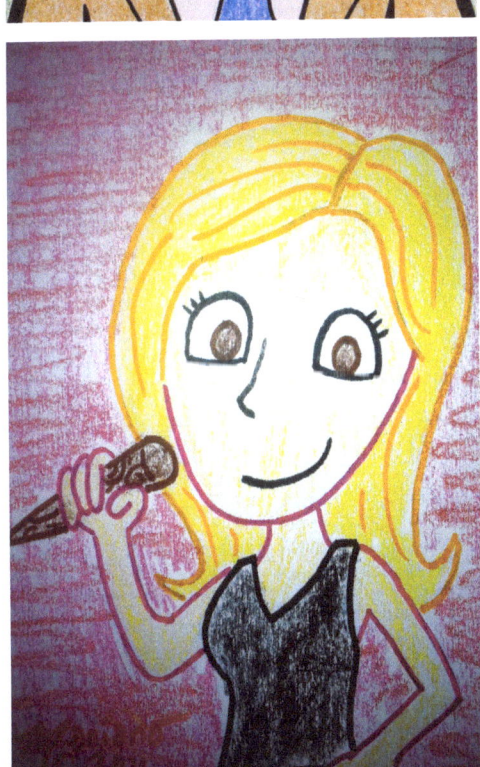
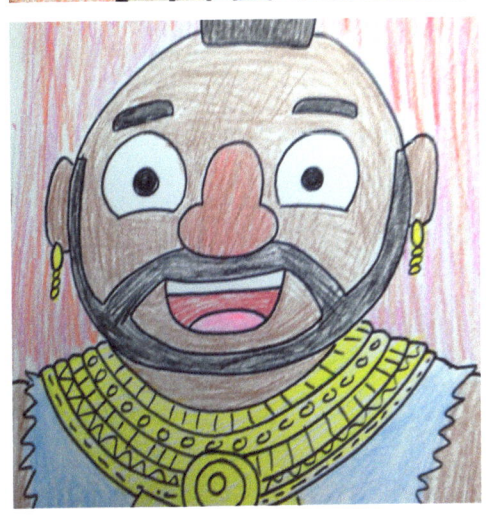

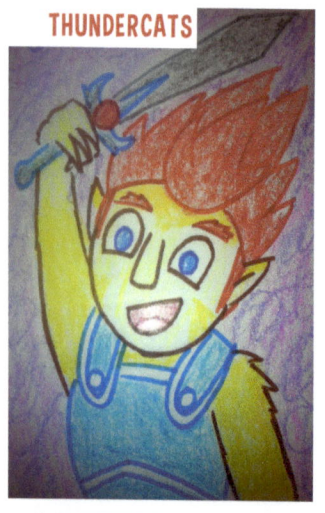
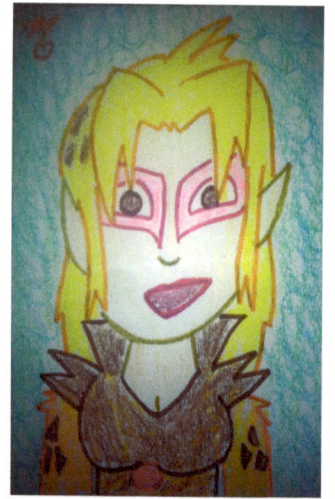
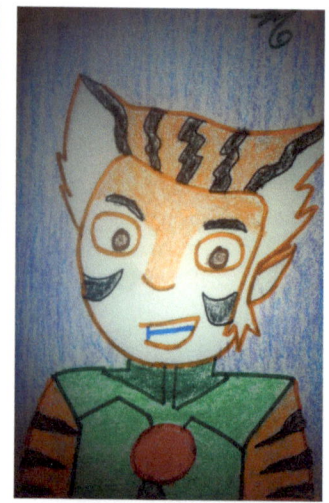
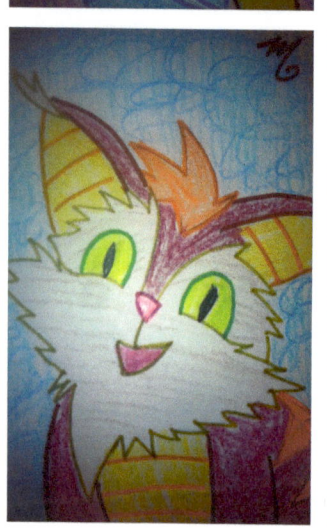

2011 ThunderCats

Lion-O
Cheetara
Tygra
Snarf
WilyKit & WilyKat
Panthro
Grune
Mumm-Ra

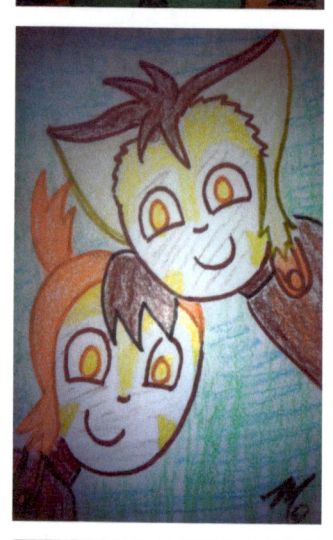
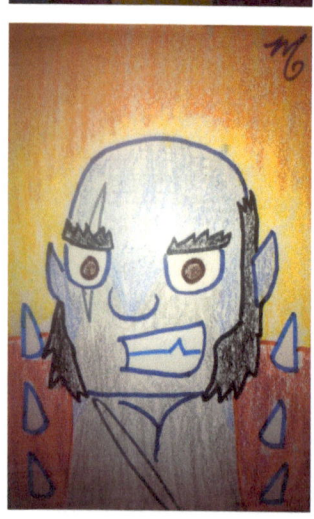
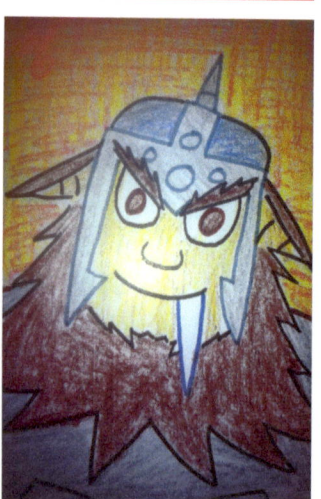
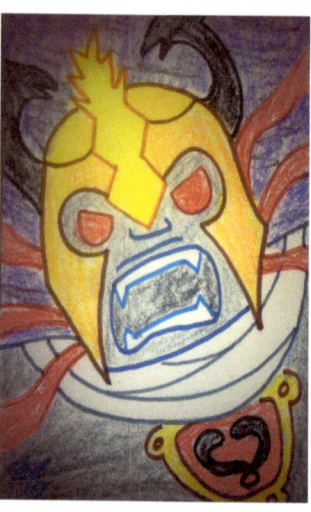

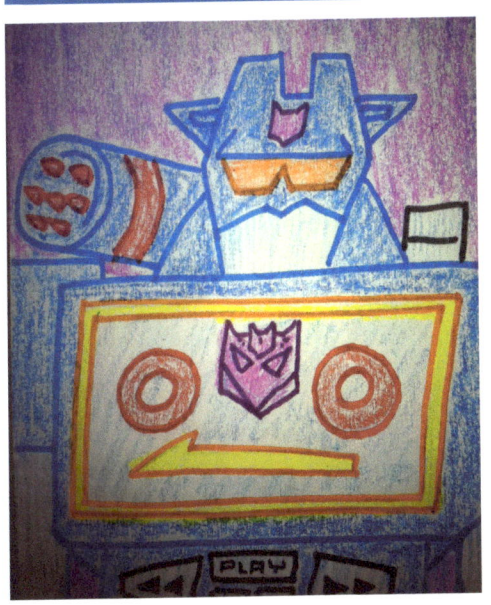

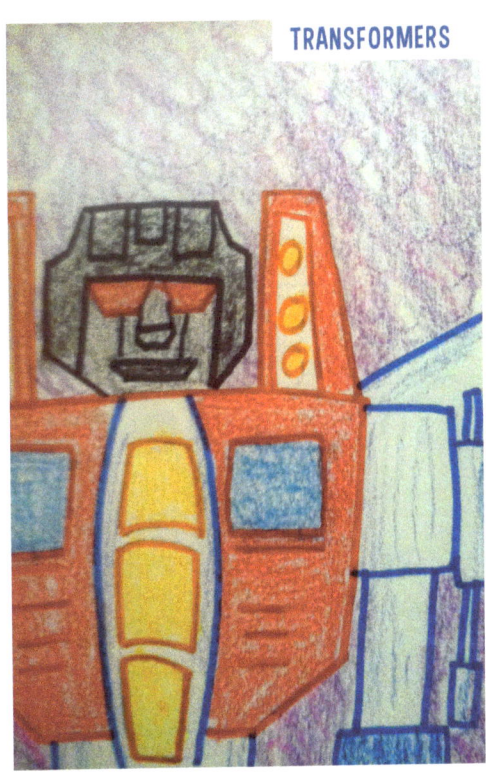

Soundwave, Starscream,
Boulder, Bumblebee, Leadfoot

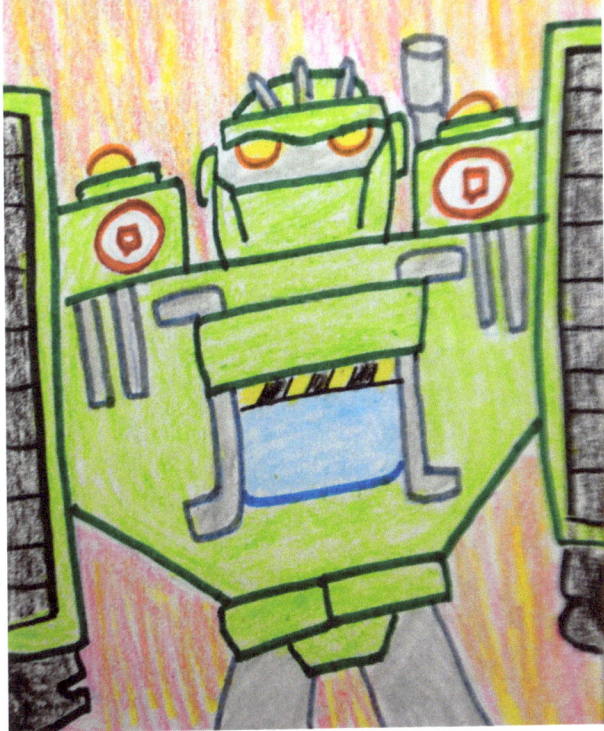

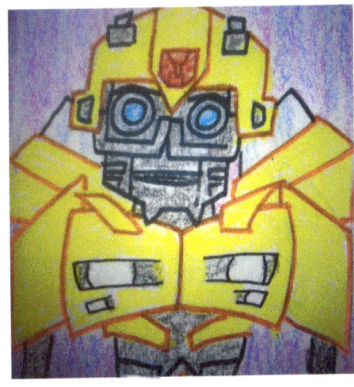

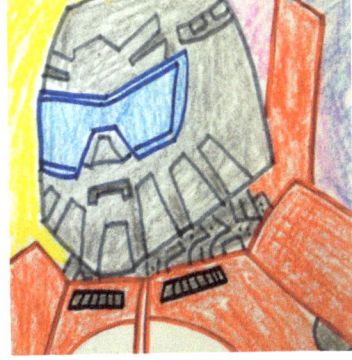

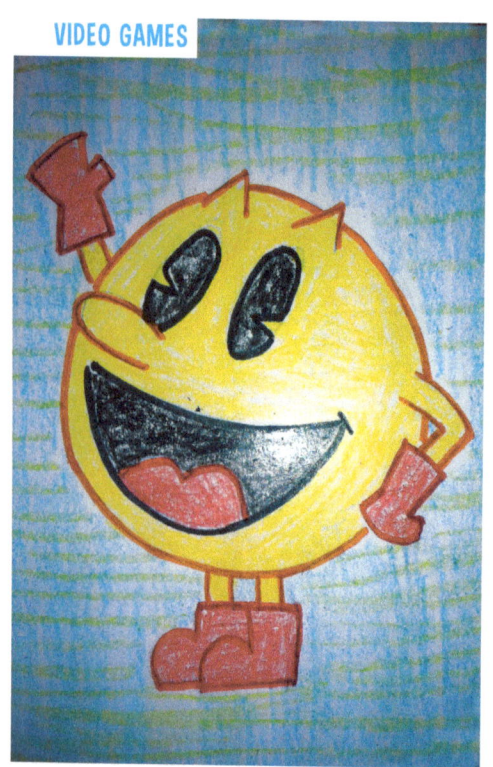

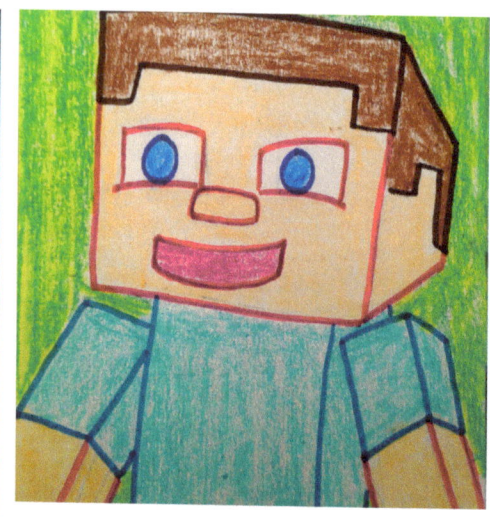

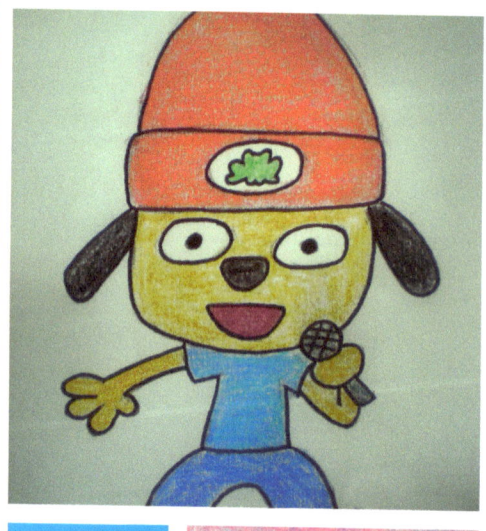

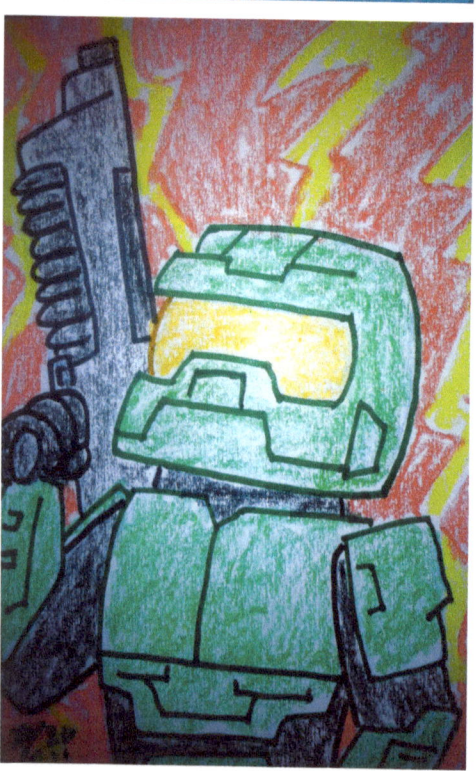

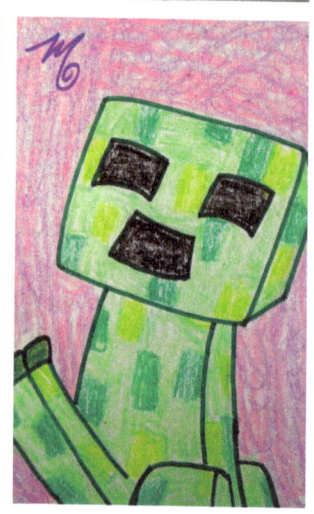

THIS PAGE:
Pac-Man
Steve
Parappa
Master Chief
Creeper

OTHER PAGE:
Ice Bird
The Prince
Sub Zero
Sackboy
Mario & Yoshi
Green Fat Bird

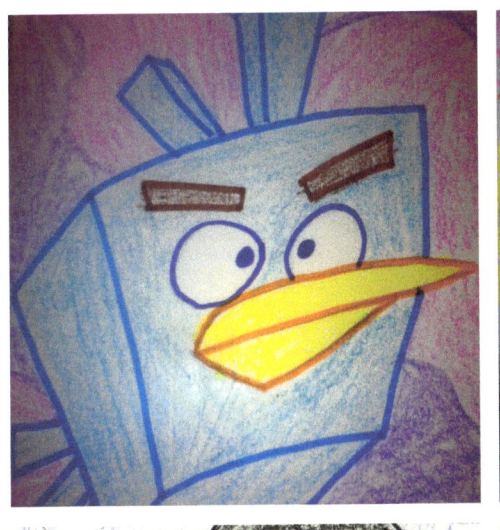
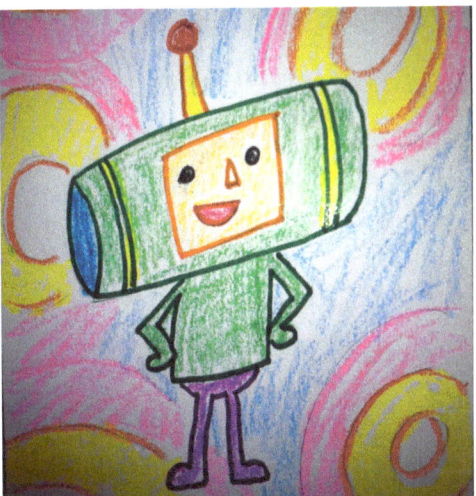
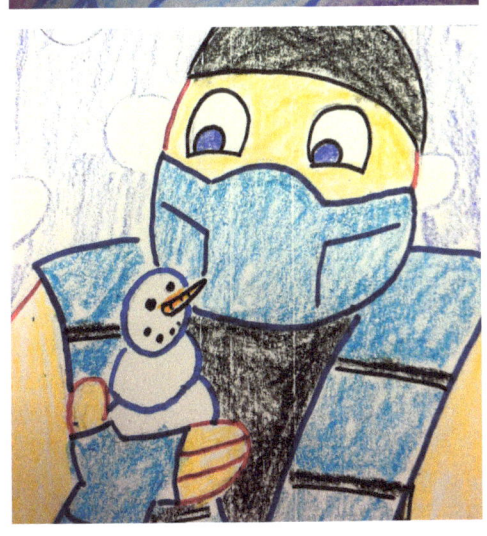
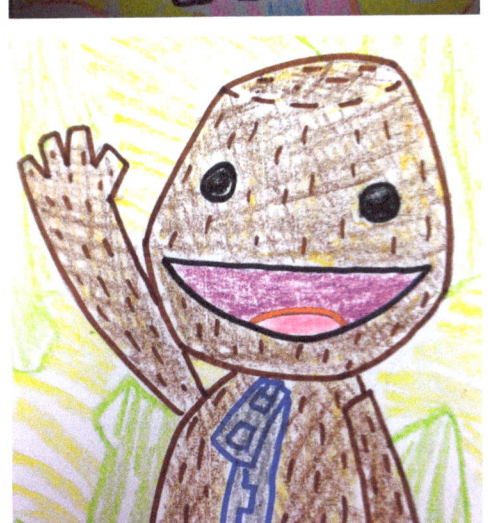
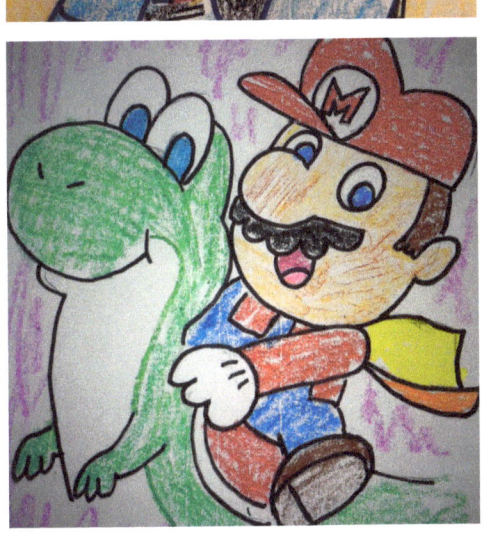
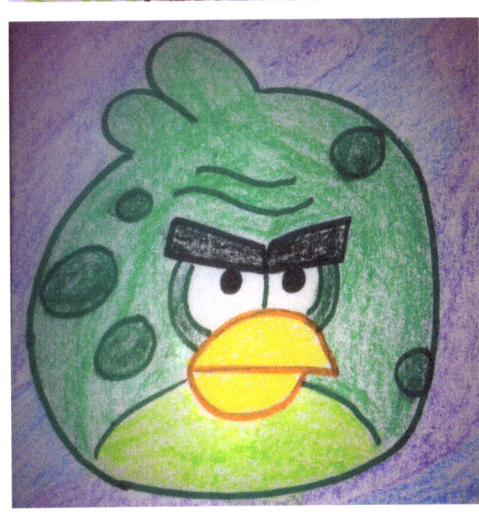

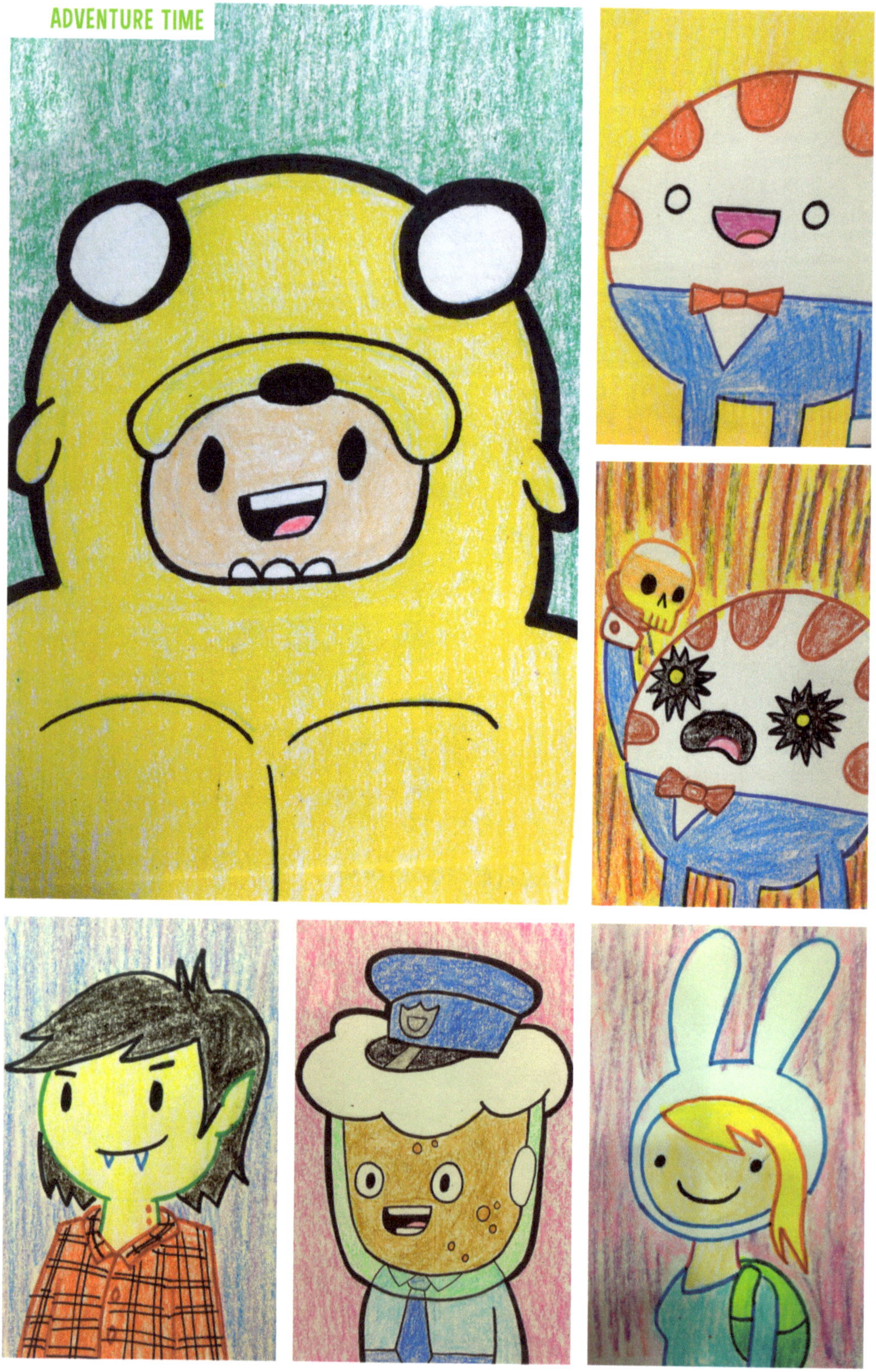

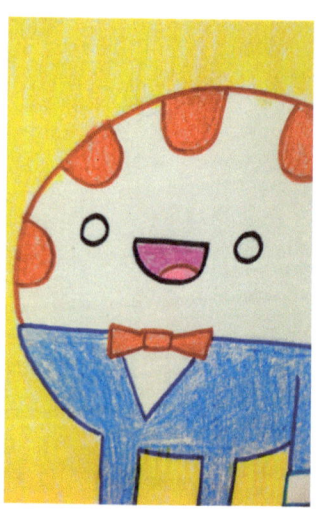

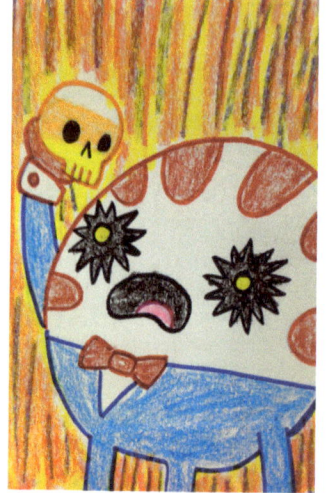

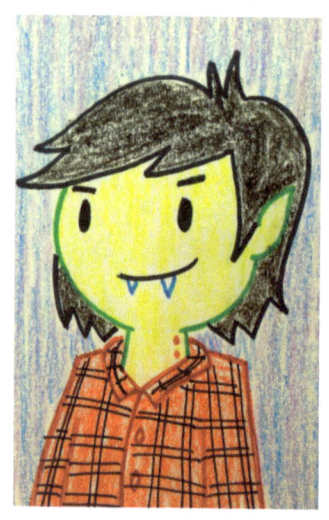

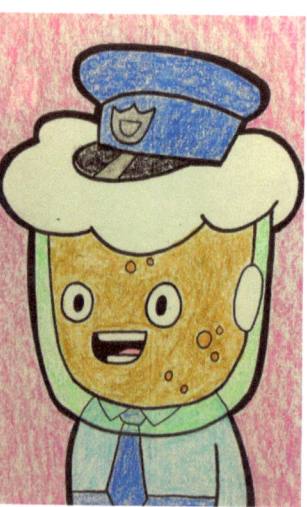

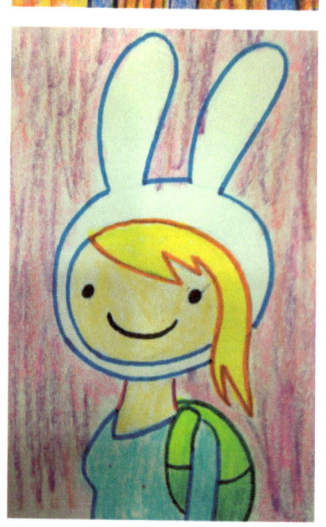

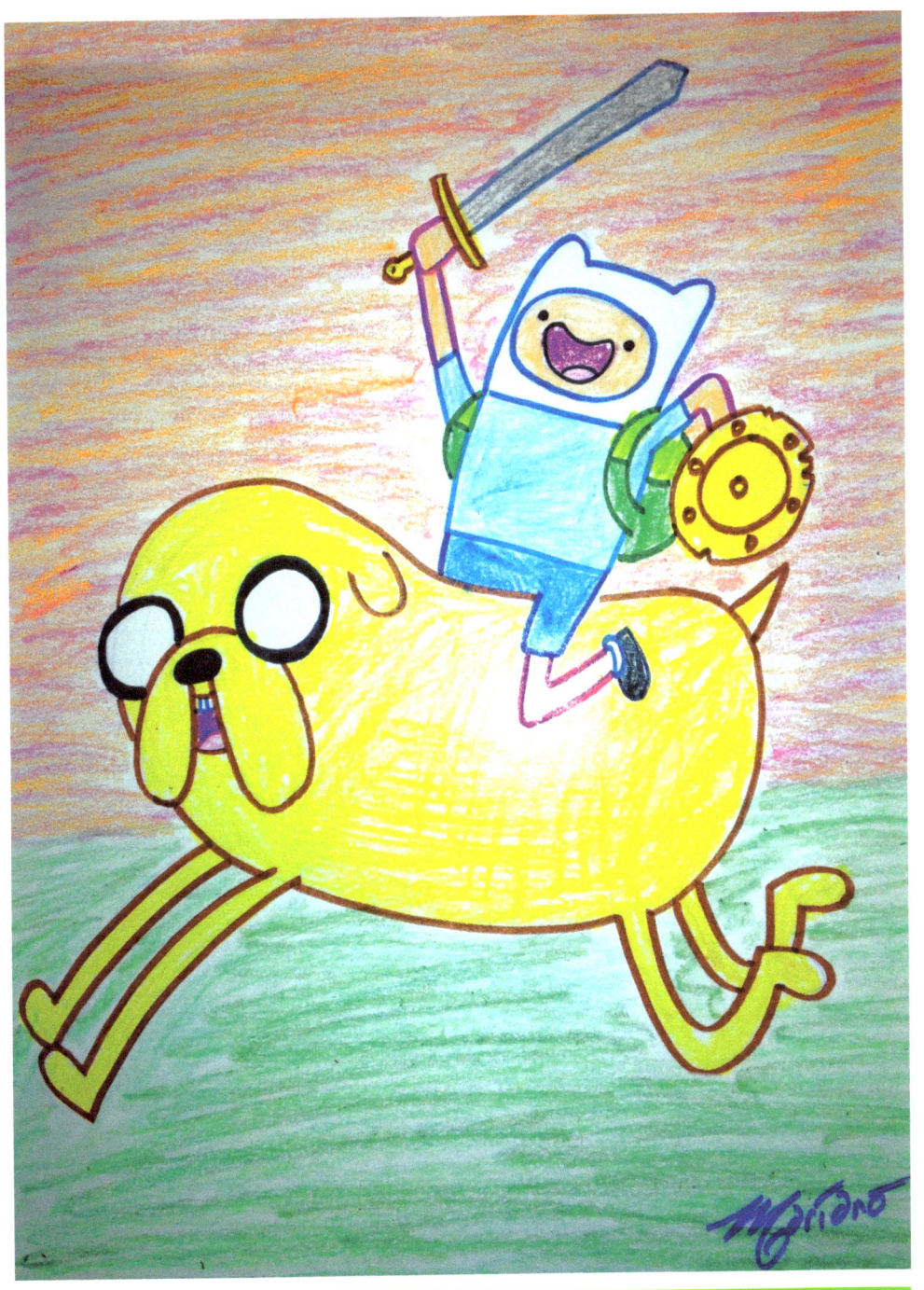

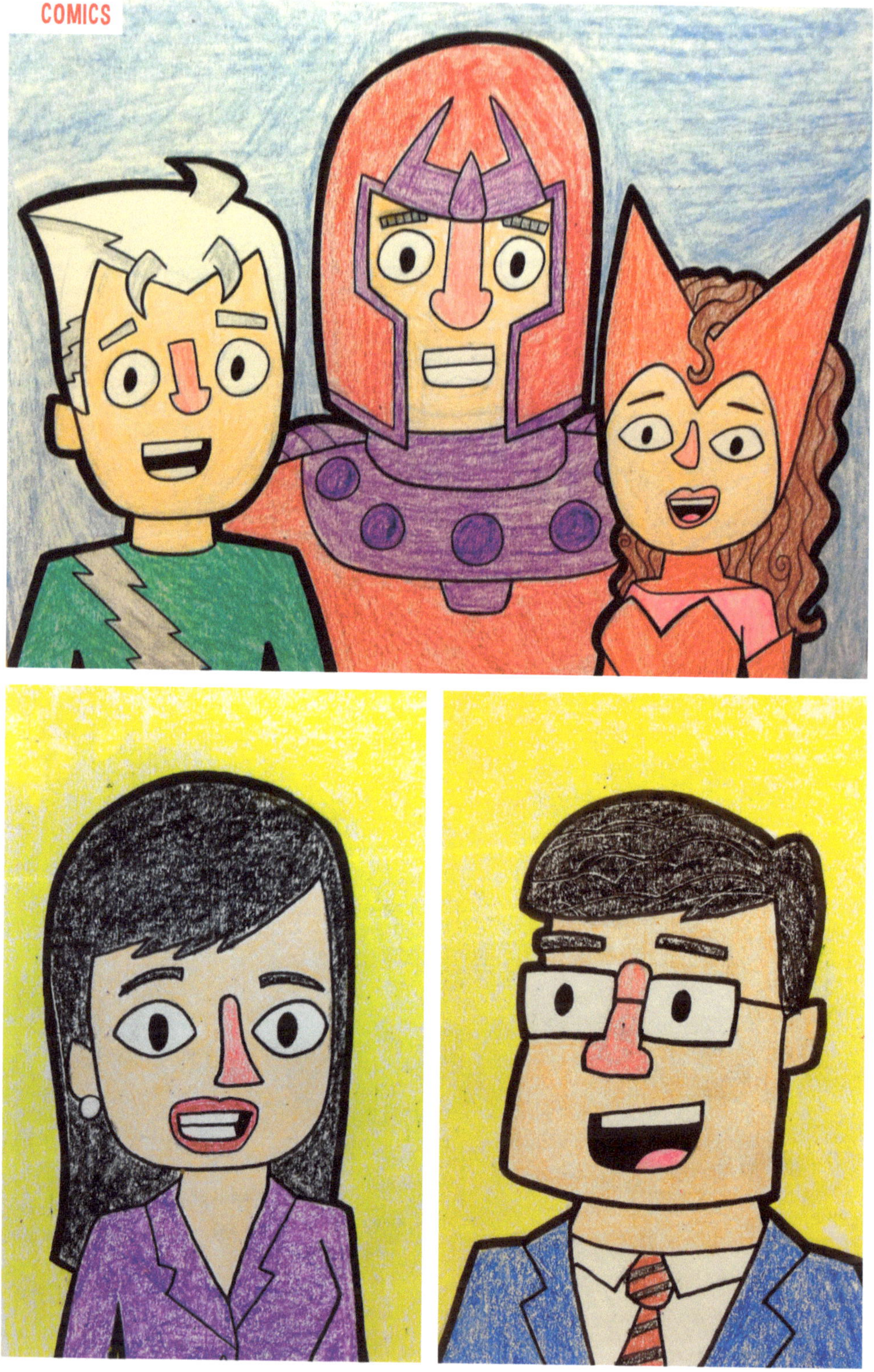

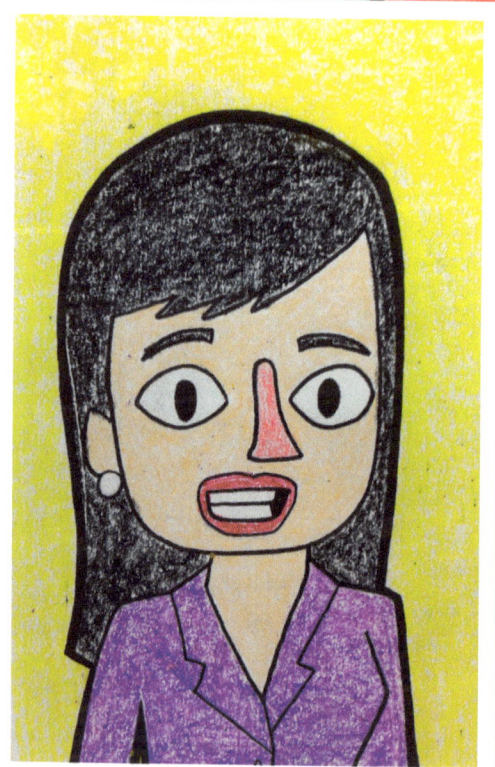
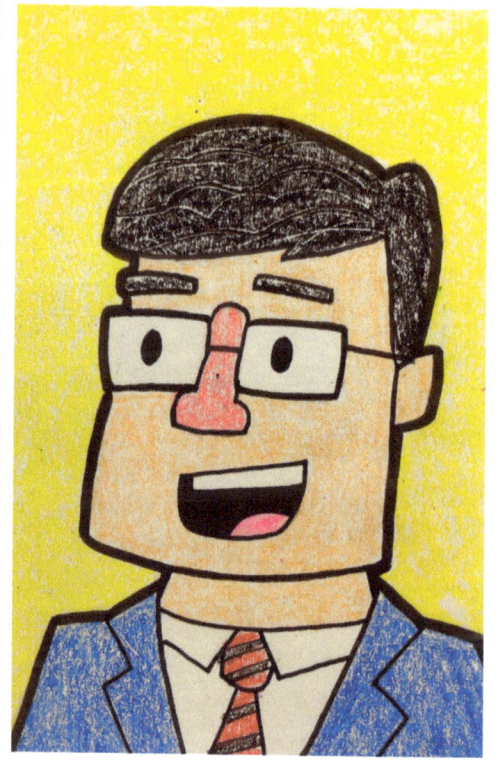

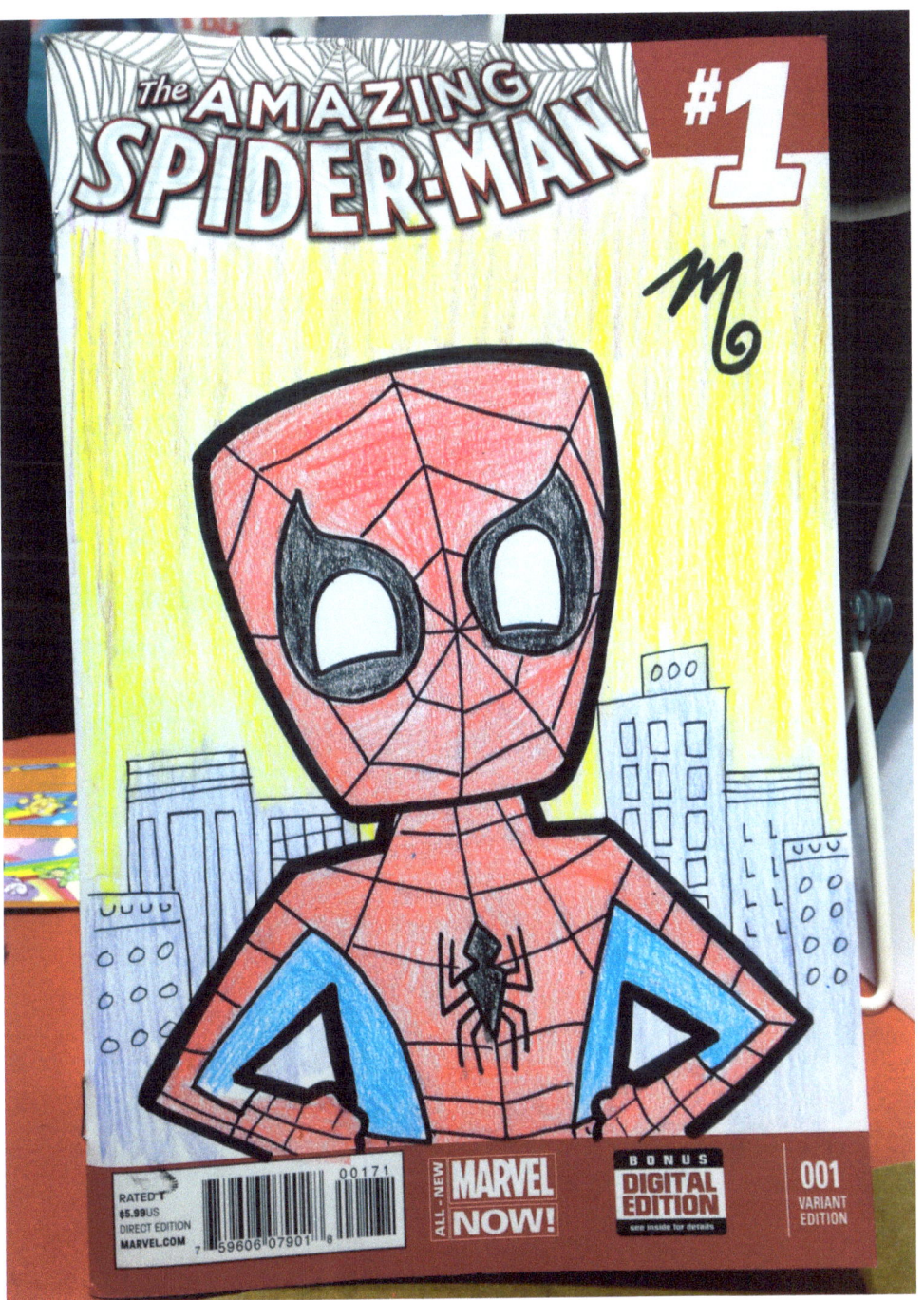

OTHER PAGE: Quicksilver, Magneto, and Scarlet Witch, Lois Lane, Clark Kent

THIS PAGE: Custom sketch cover: Spider-Man

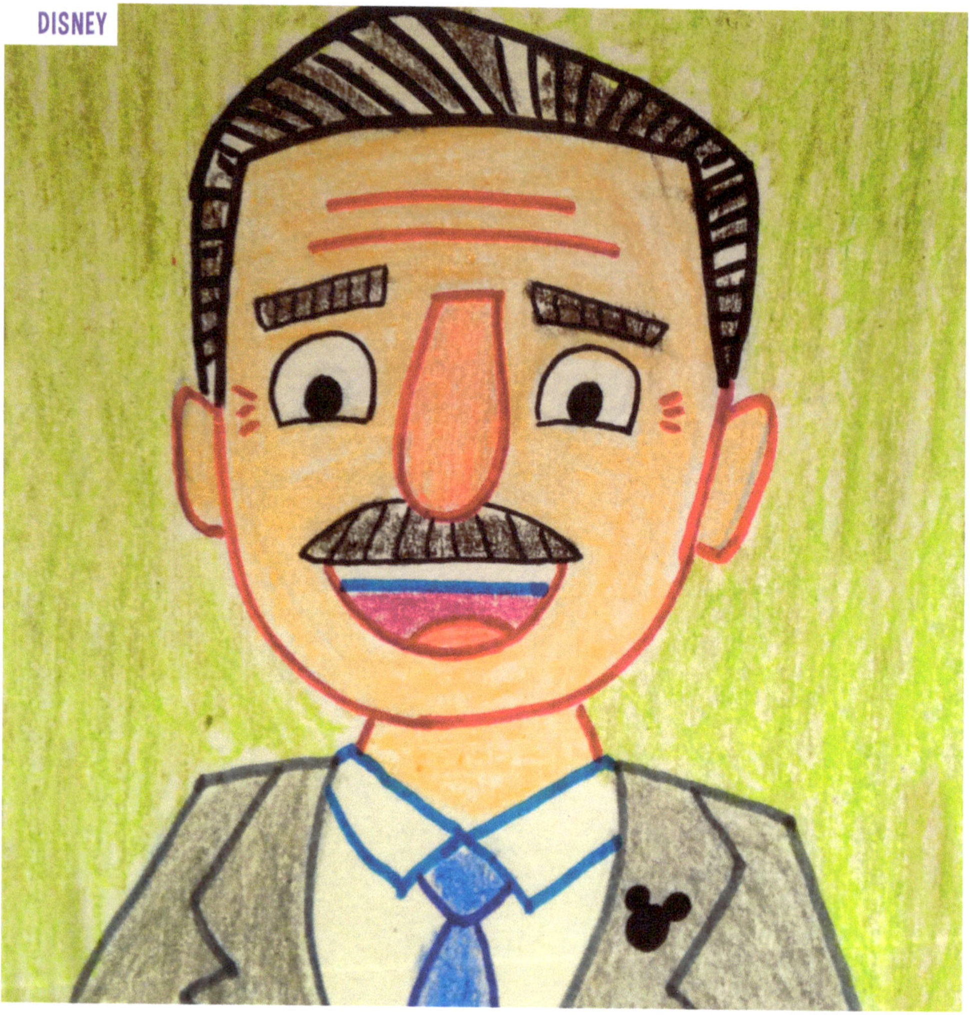

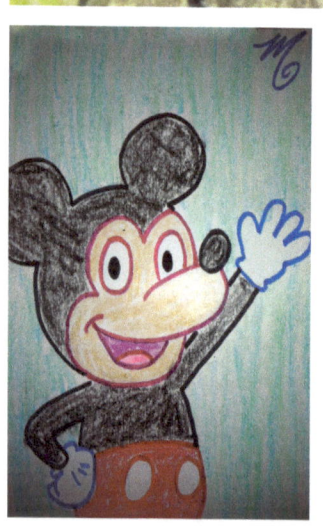
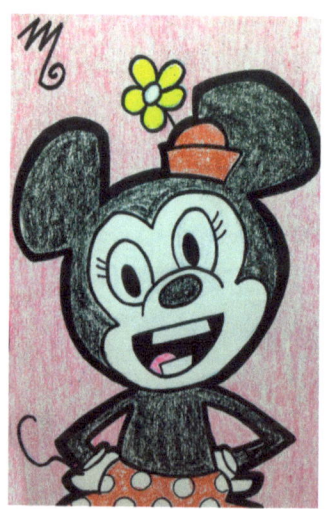
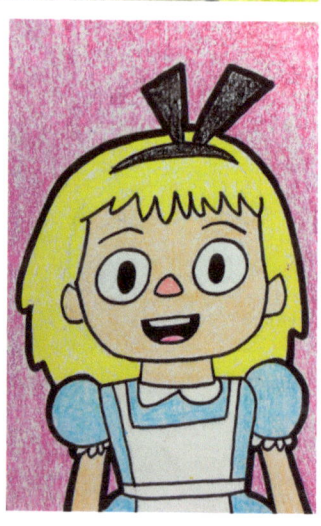

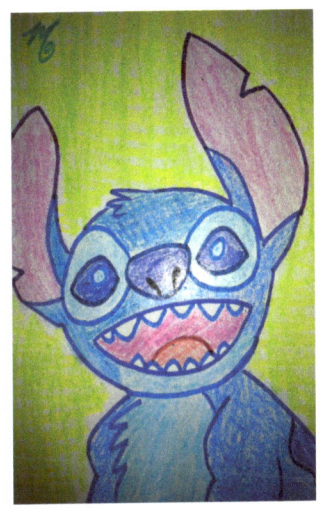
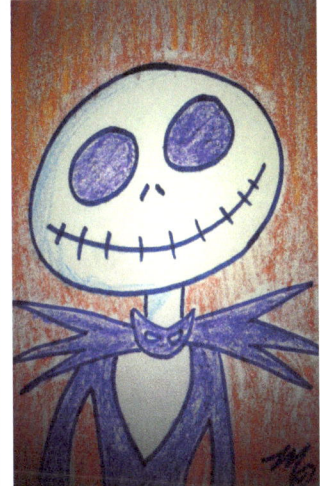
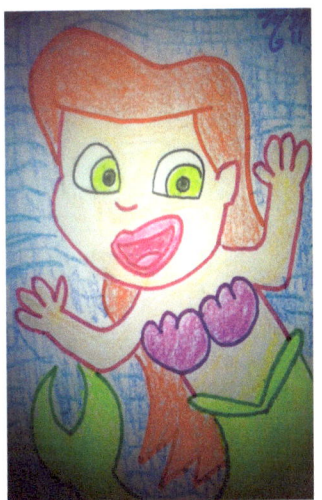

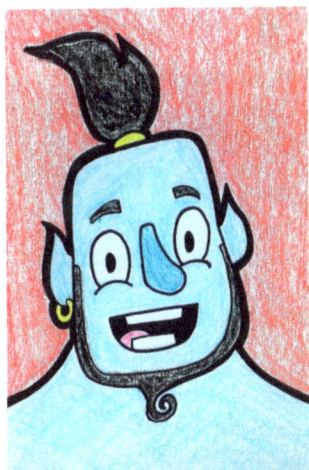
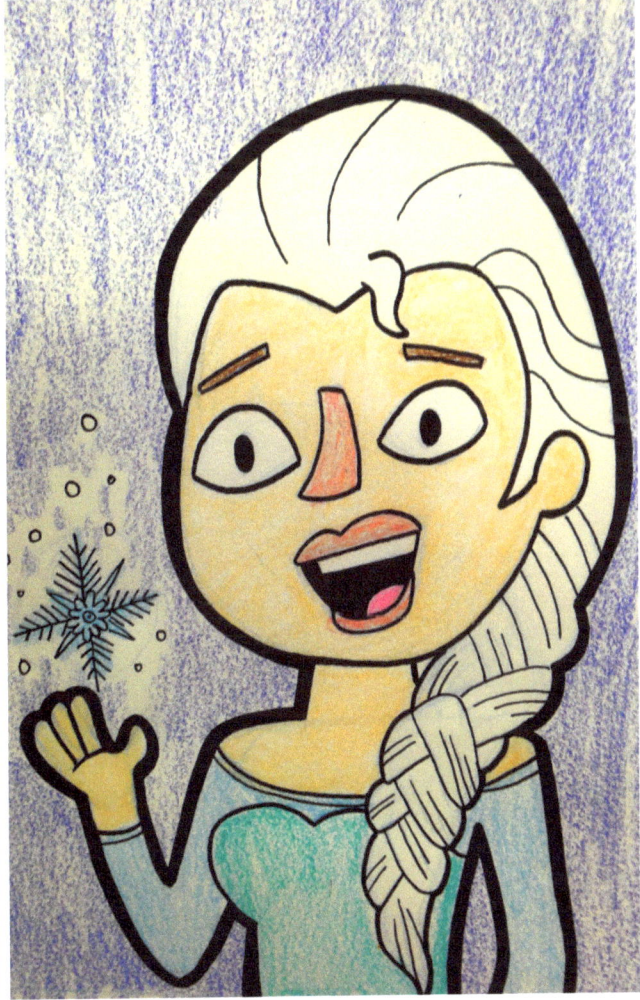

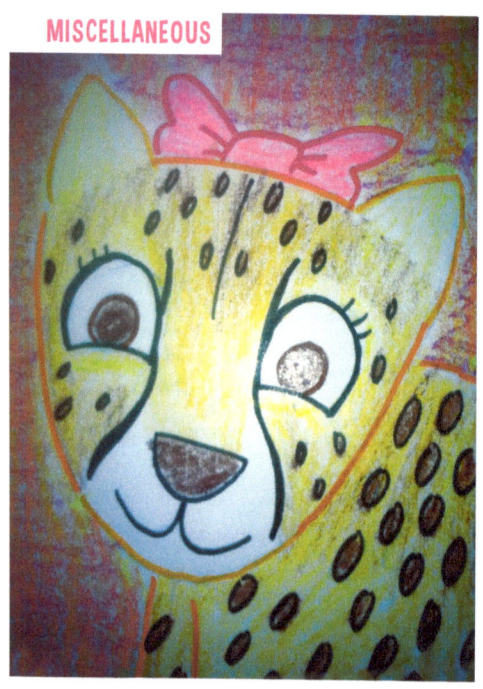

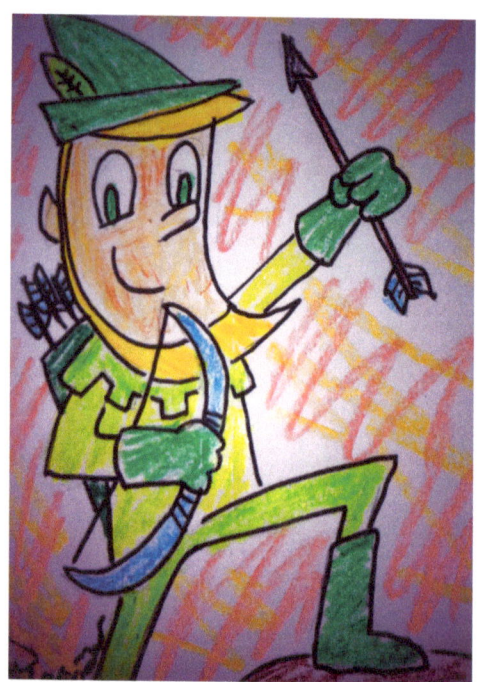

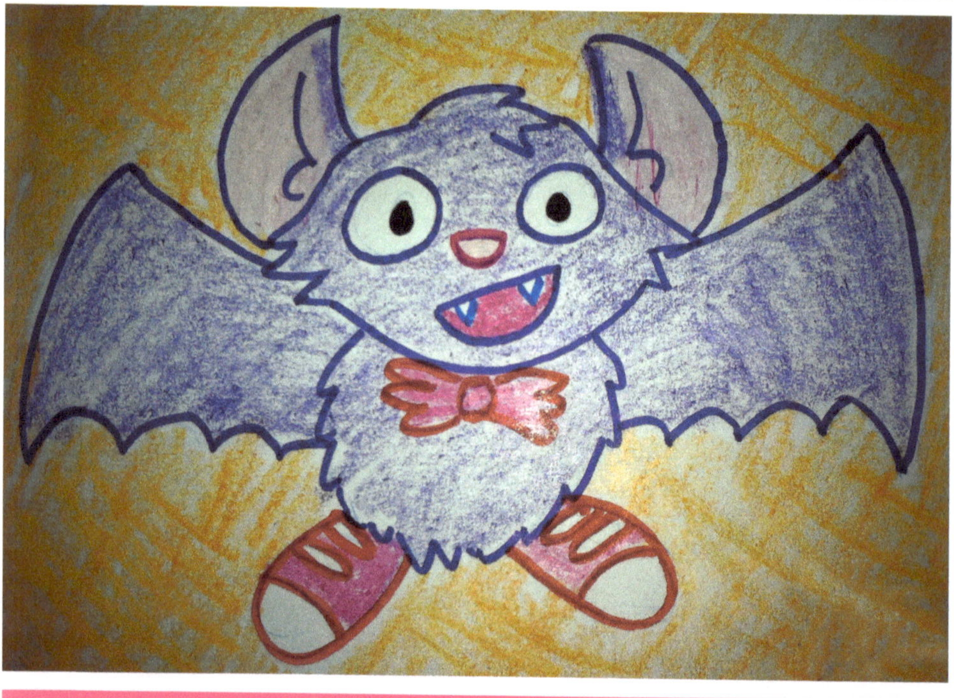

THIS PAGE: Cheetah With a Bow, Robin Hood, Bow Tie Bat

OTHER PAGE: Kool-Aid Man, Tomato Juice Spider, Sneaker Blue Bird

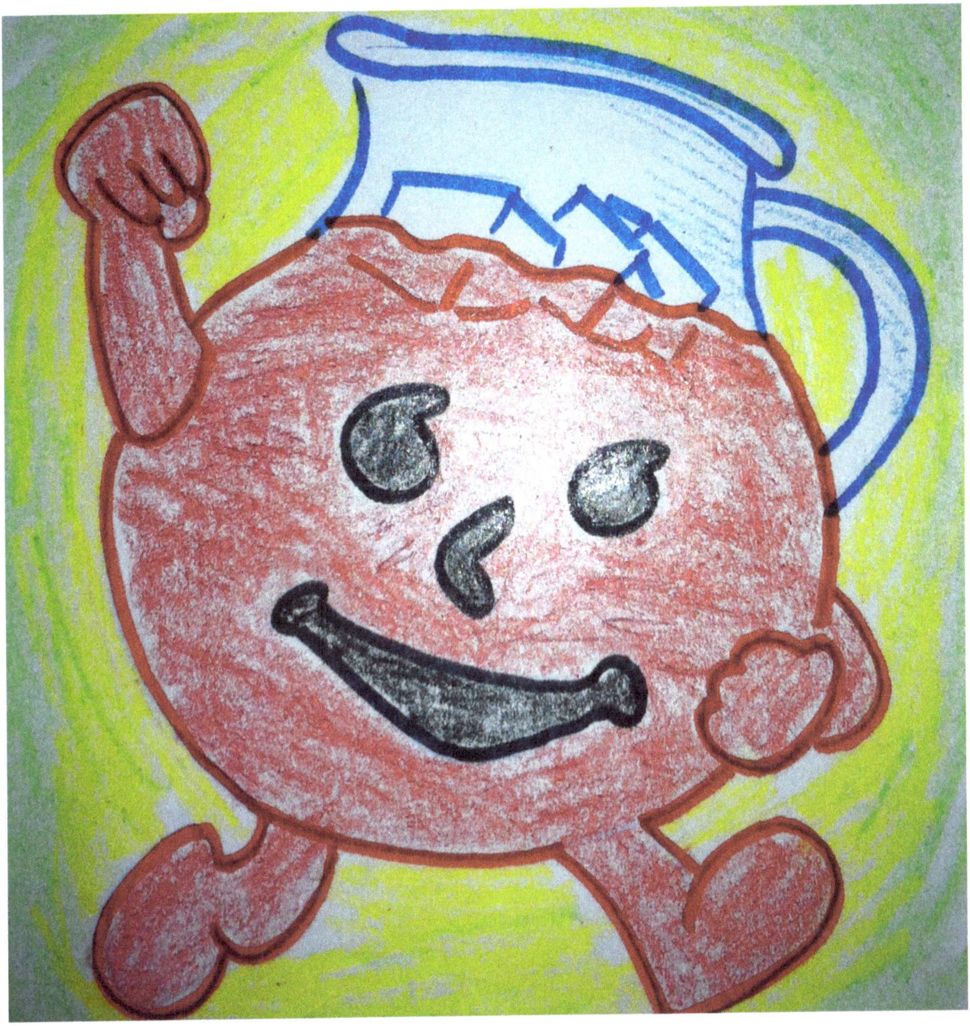

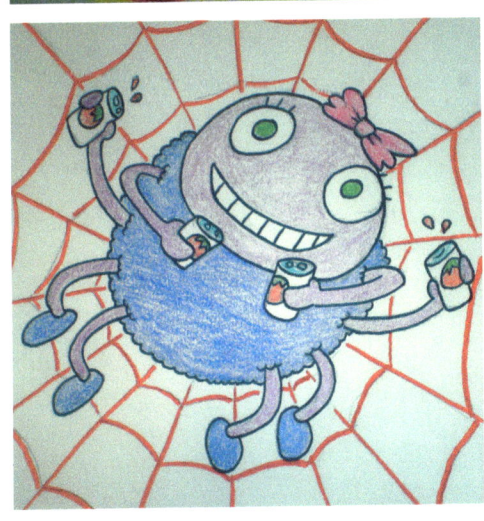

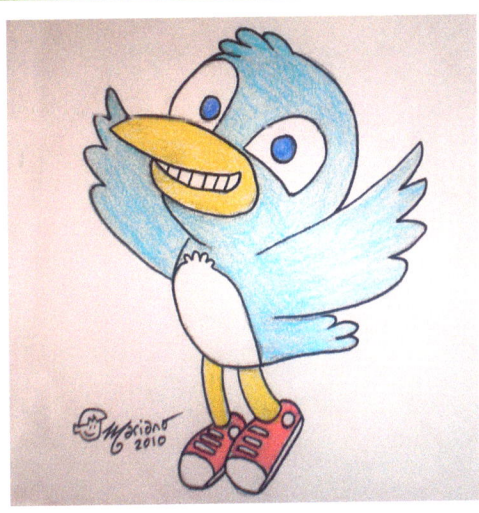

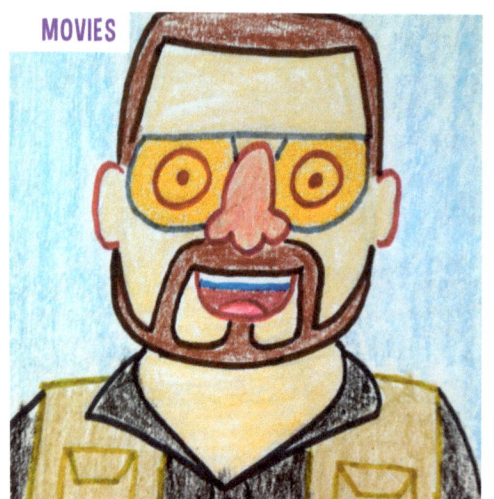

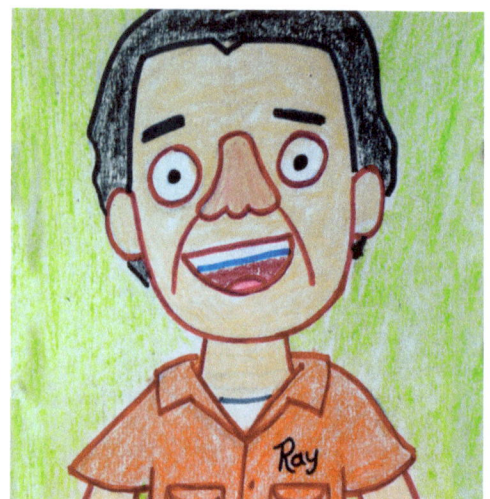

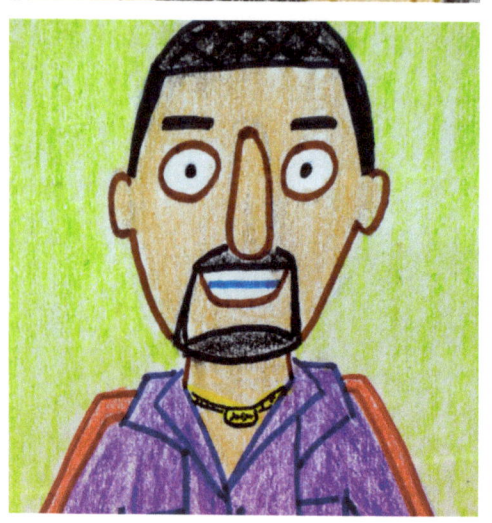

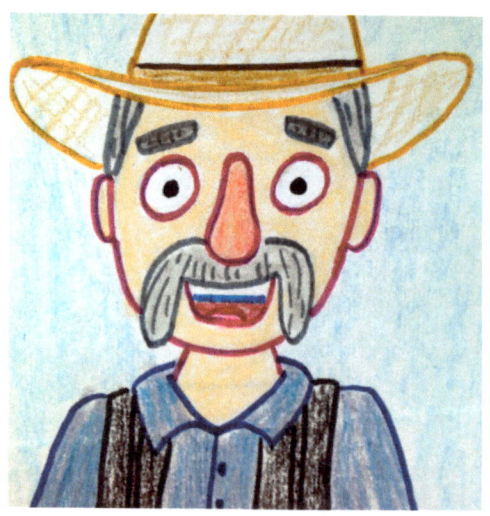

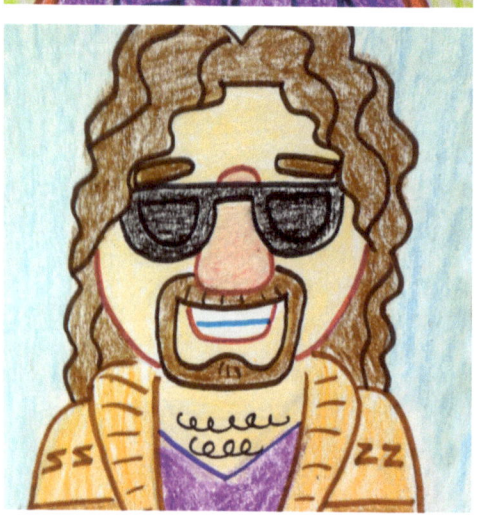

THIS PAGE:
The Big Lebowski:
Walter, Donny, Jesus,
The Stranger, The Dude

OTHER PAGE:
Kill Bill:
The Bride, Gogo Yubari, Elle Driver,
Copperhead, O-Ren Ishii,
Sidewinder, Bill

Groundhog Day

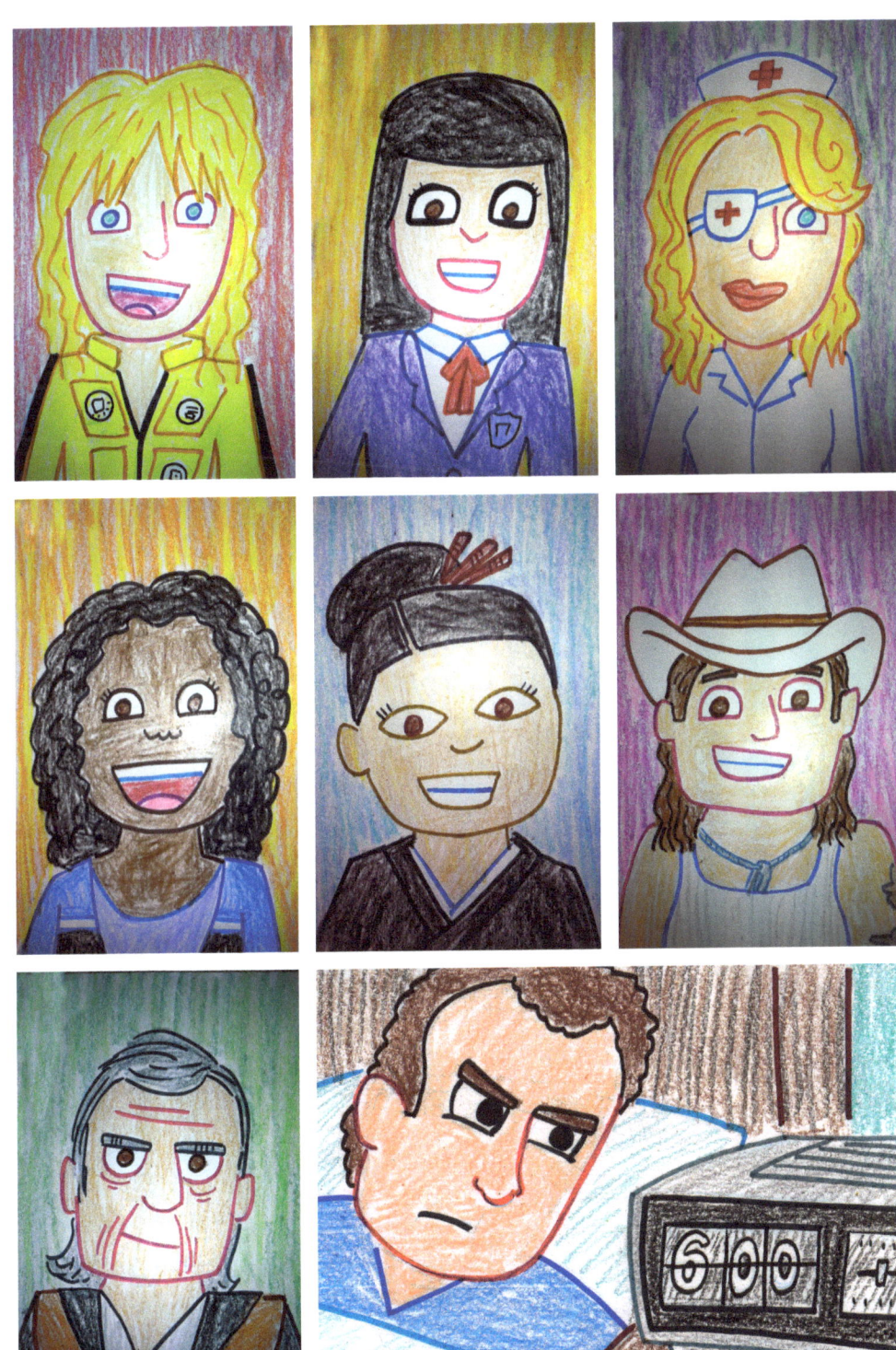

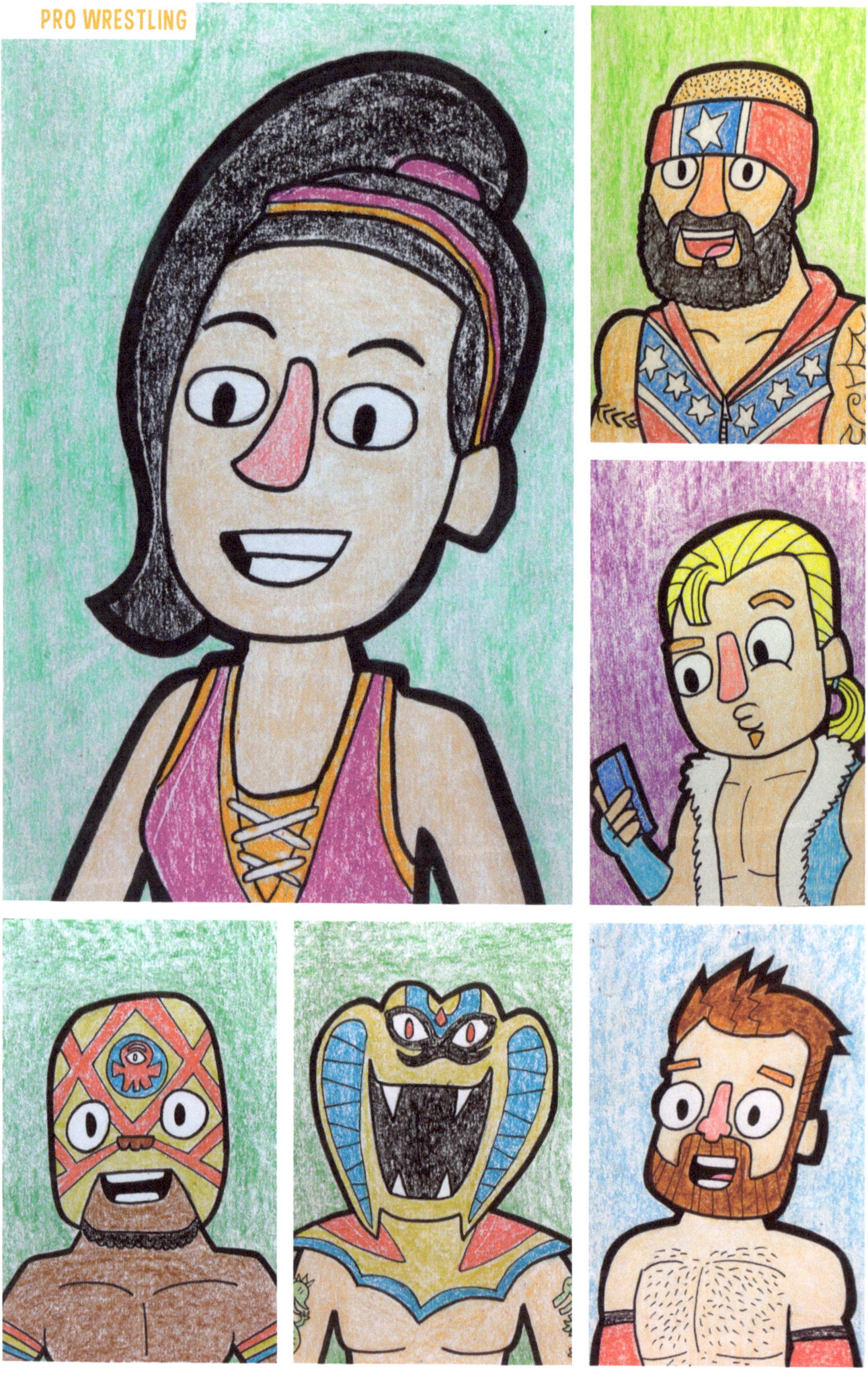

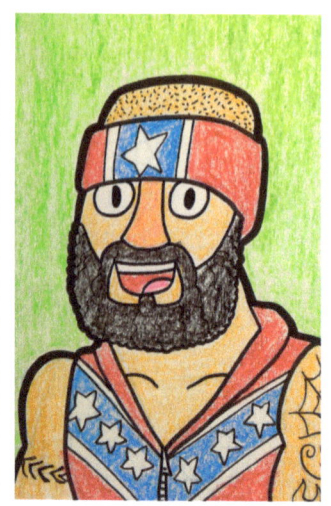
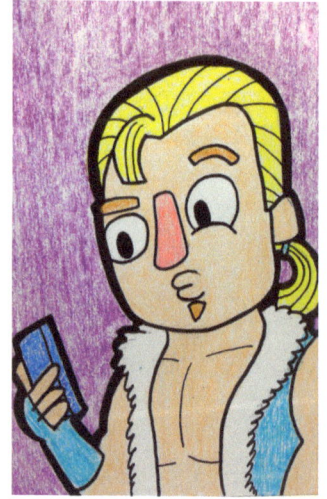
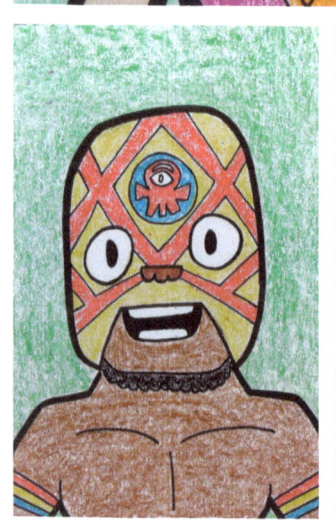
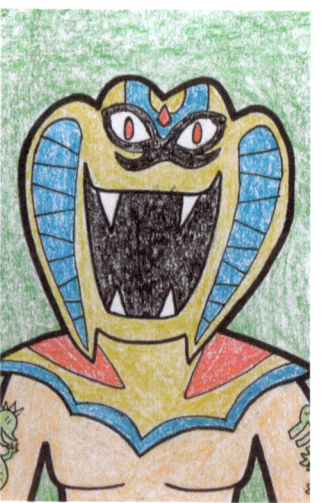
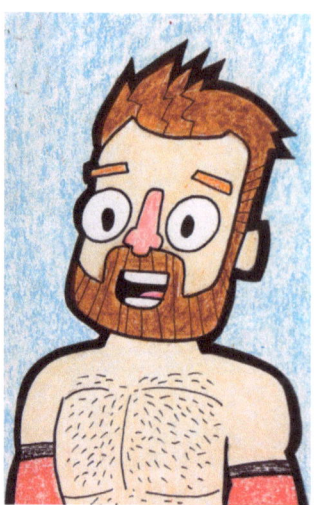

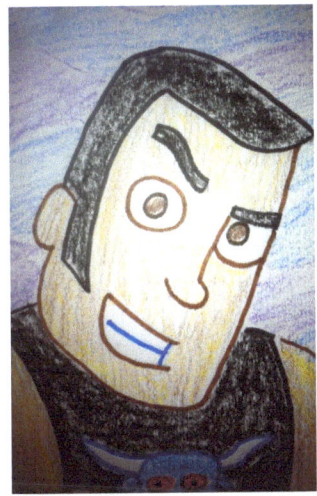

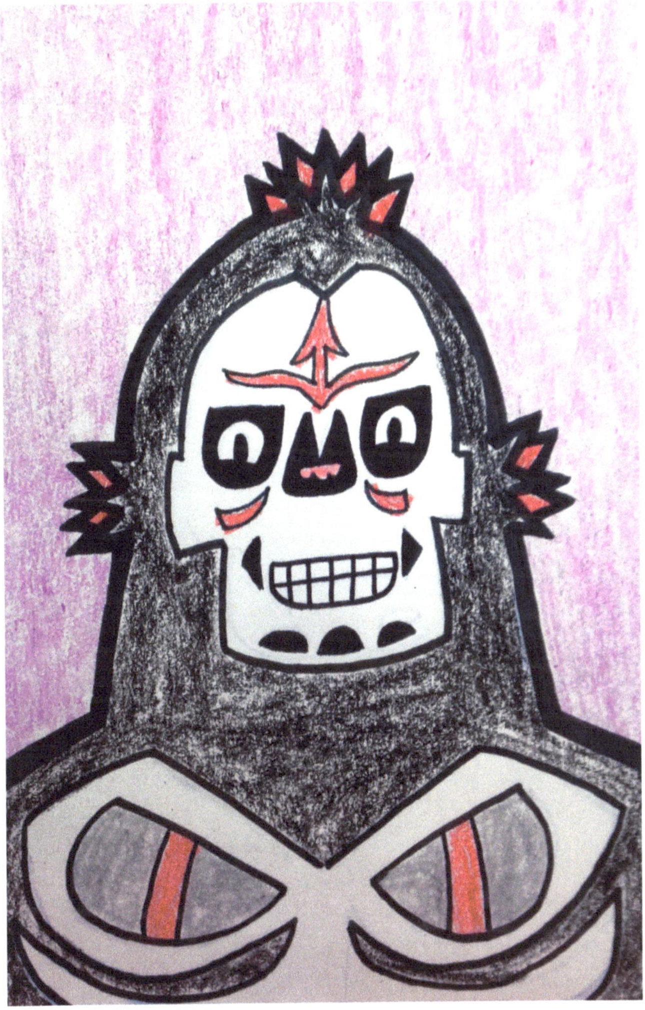

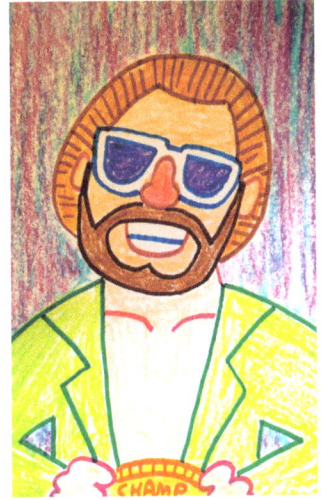

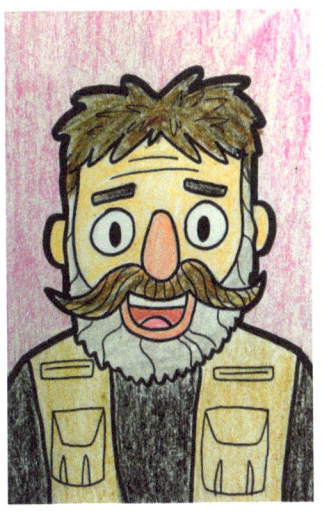

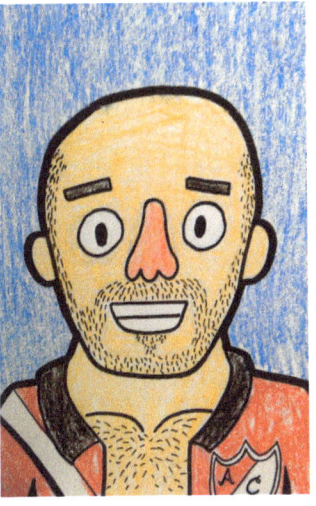

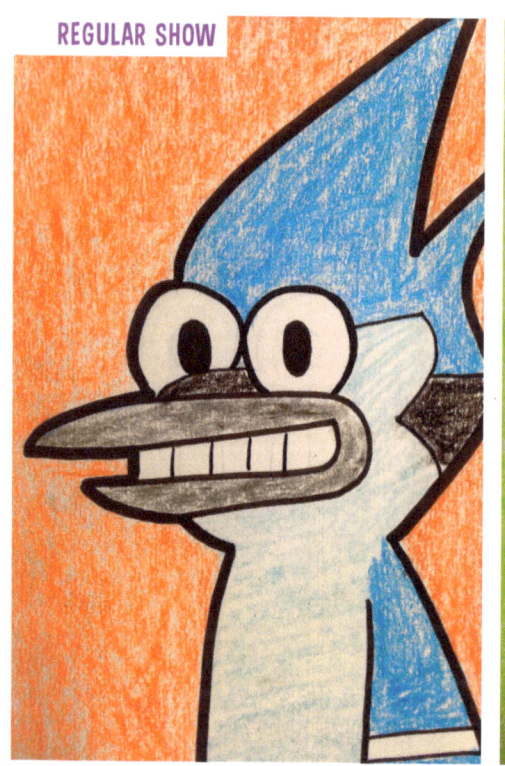
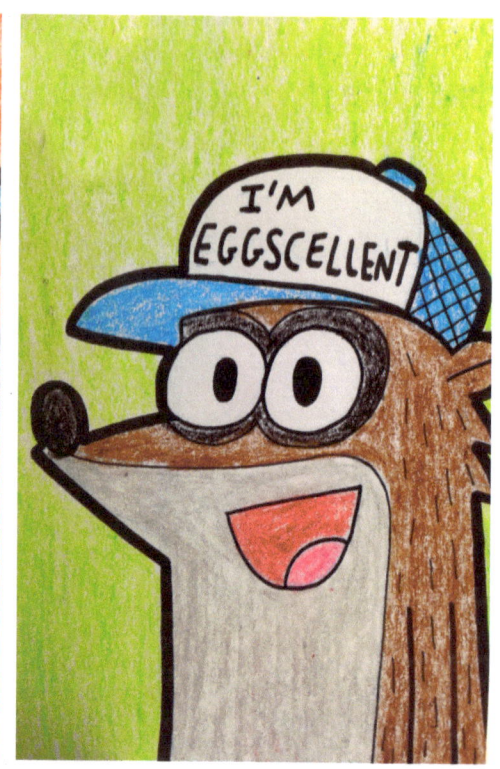
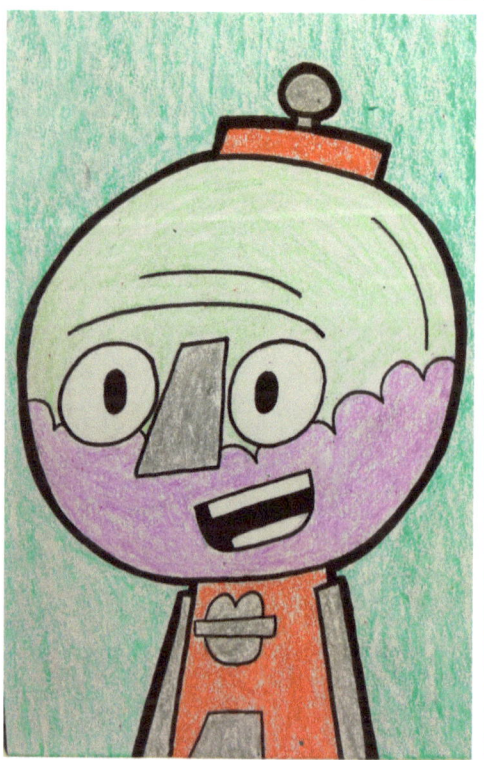
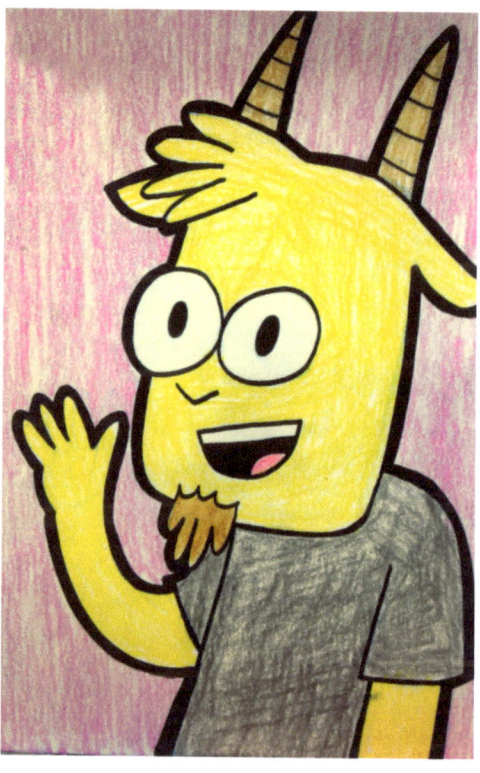

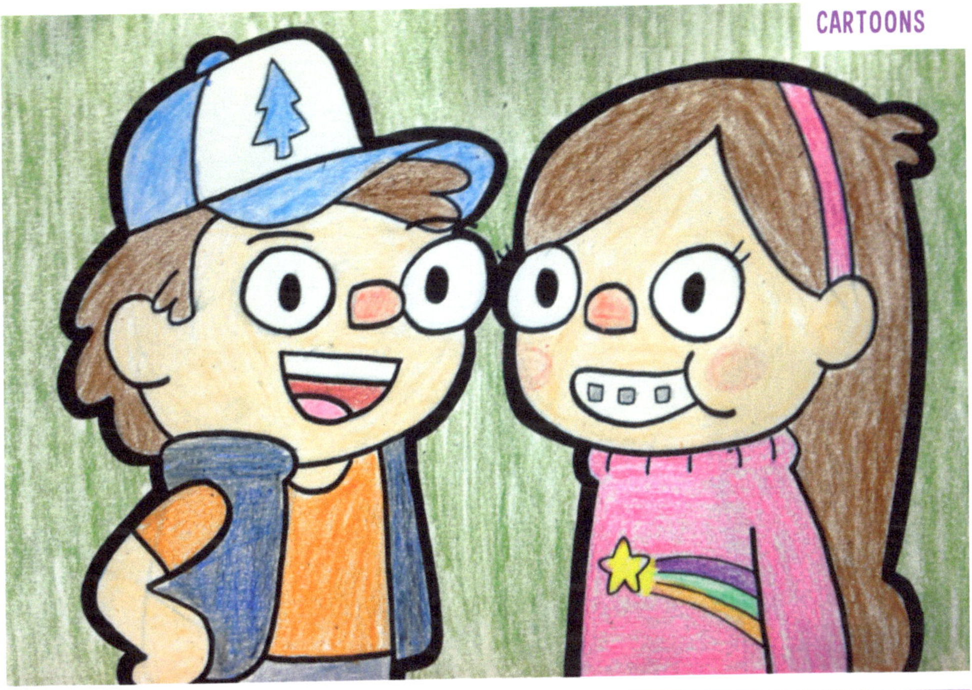

OTHER PAGE: Mordecai, Rigby, Benson, Thomas

THIS PAGE: Dipper and Mabel, Gumball and Darwin

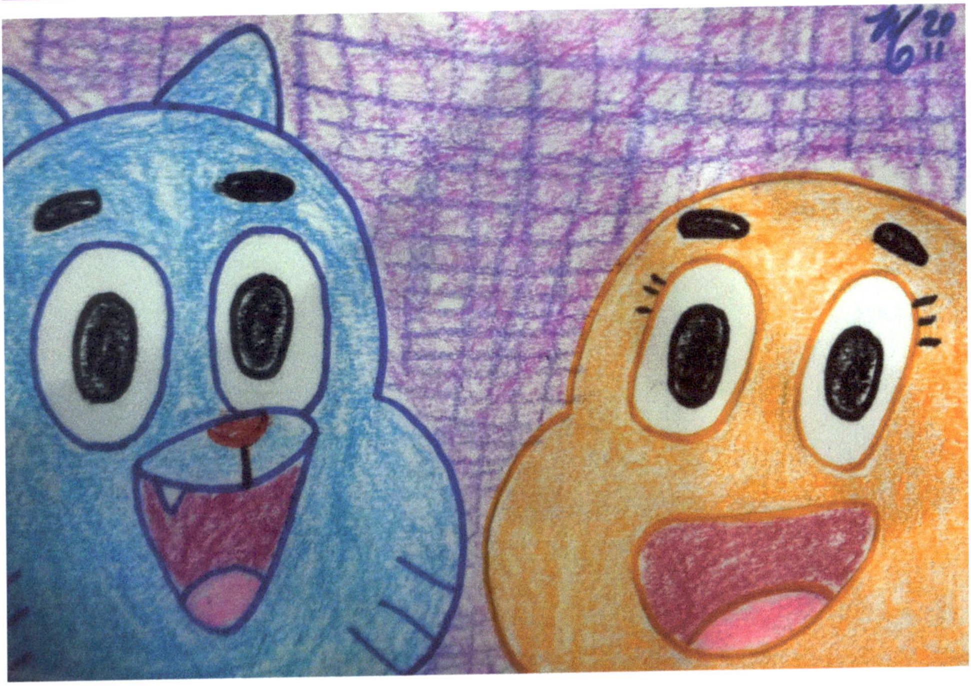

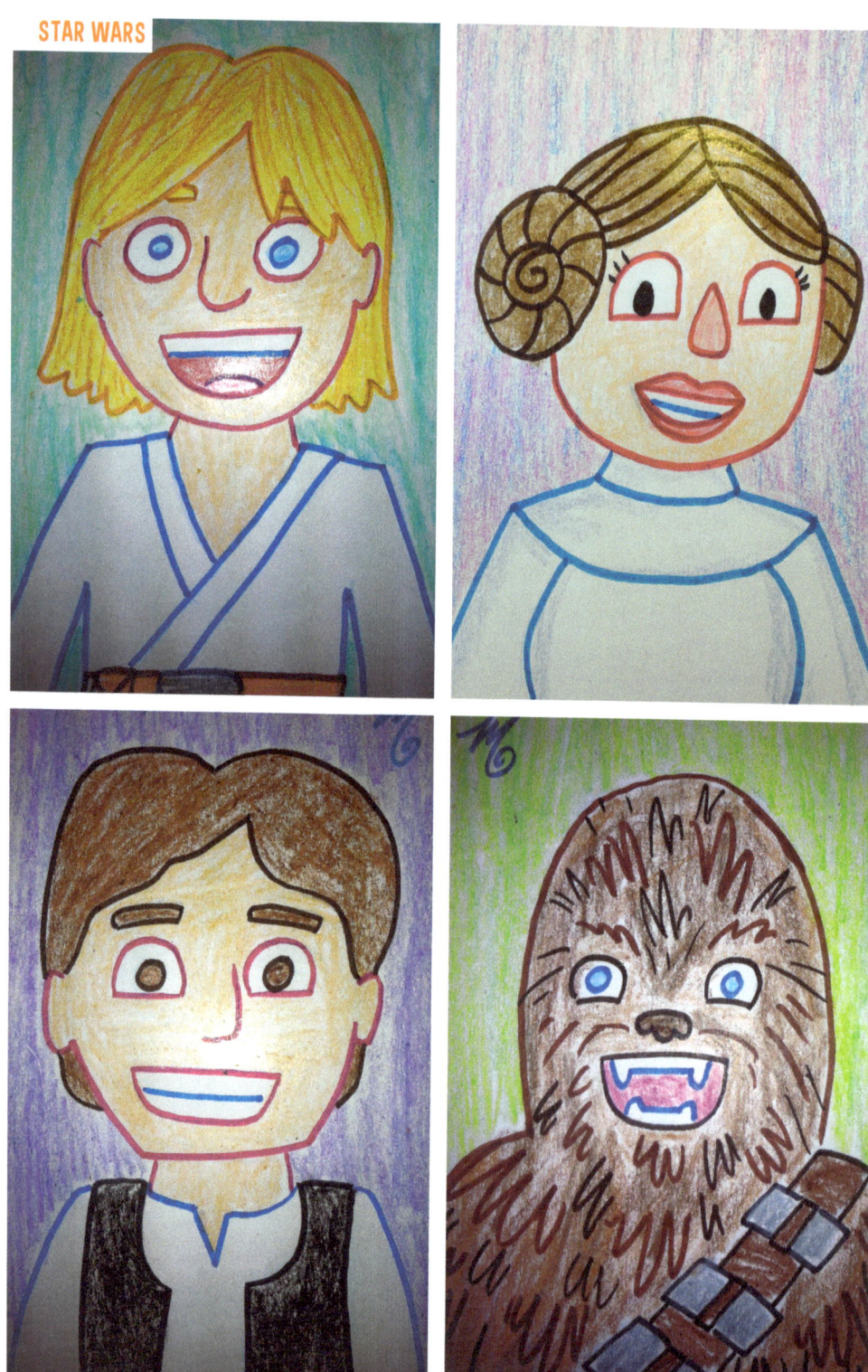

OTHER PAGE:
Luke Skywalker
Princess Leia
Han Solo
Chewbacca

THIS PAGE:
Pilot Luke
Obi Wan Kenobi
Jawa
Rebel Leia
Darth Vader

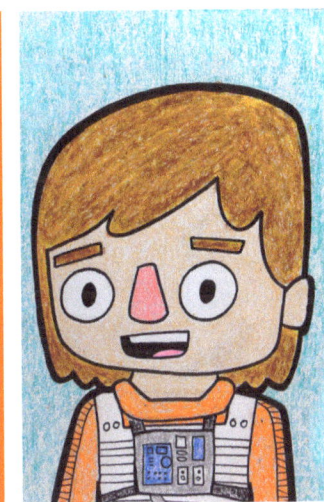

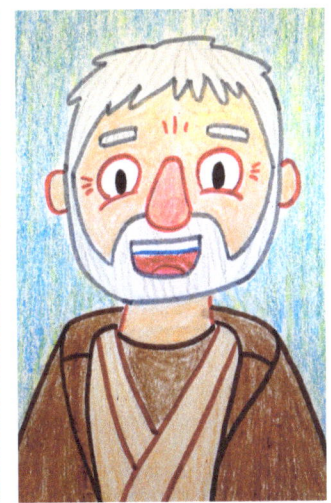

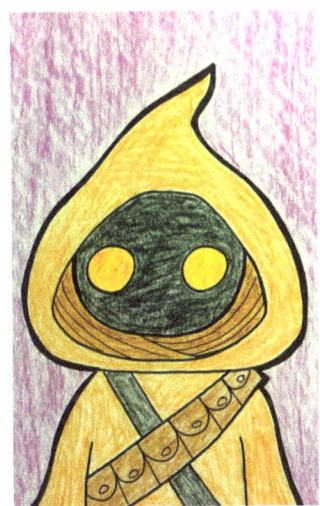

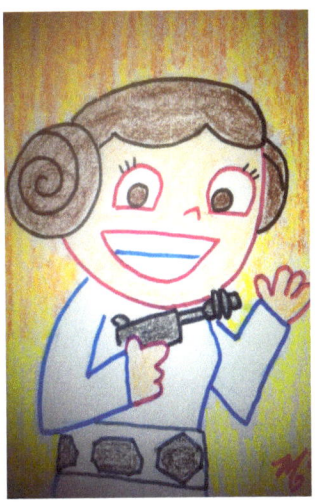

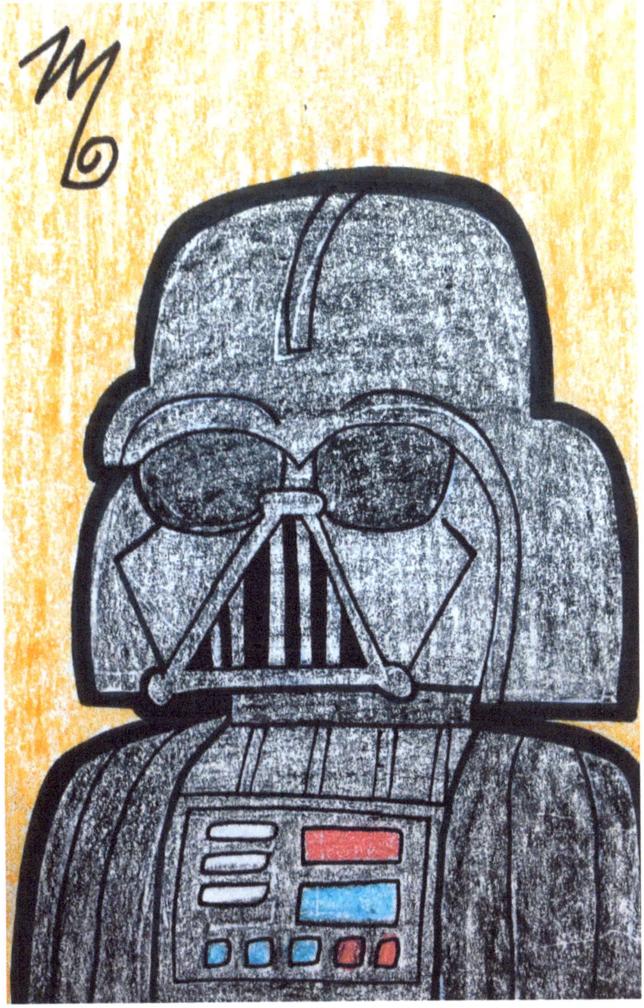

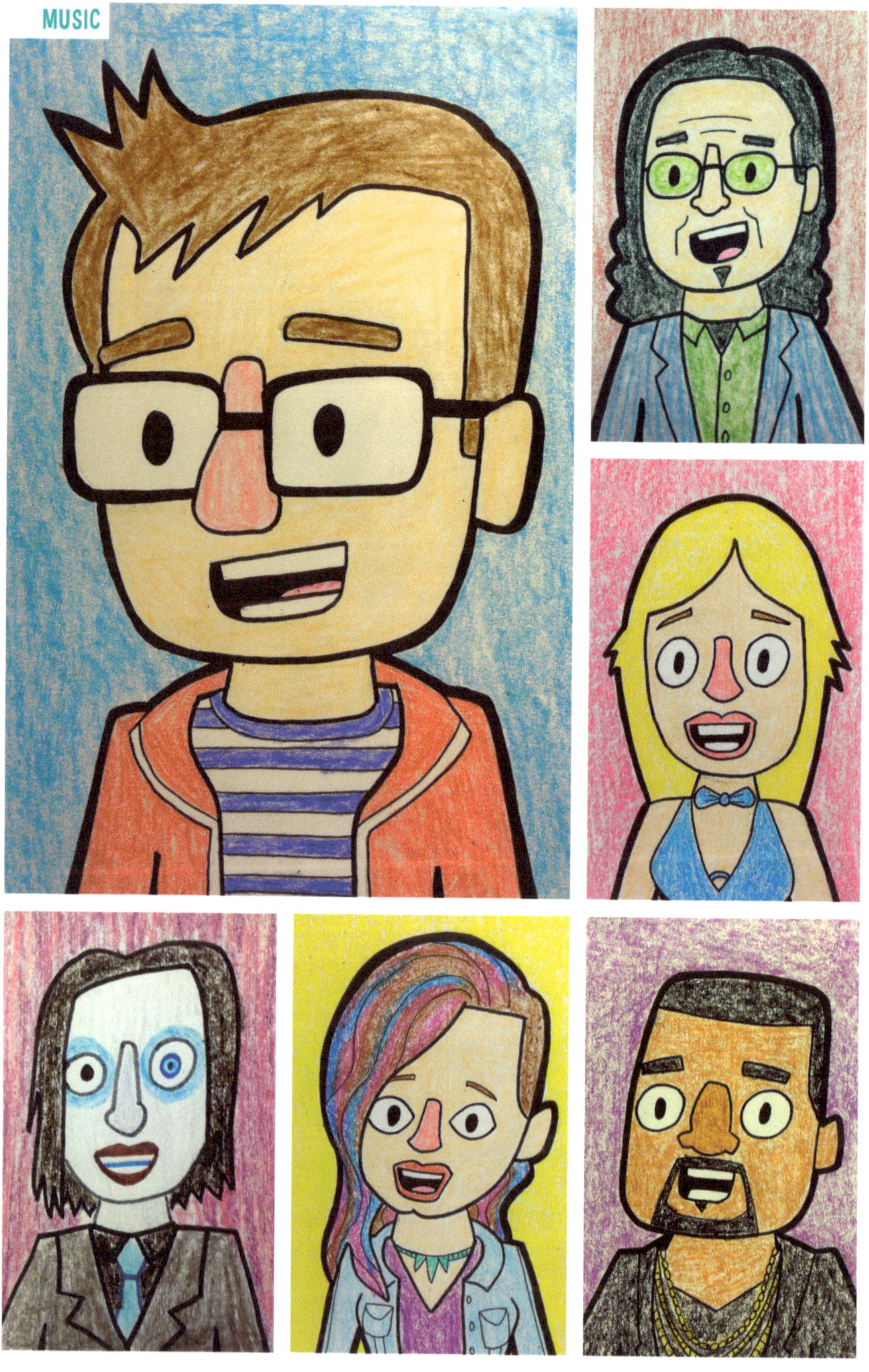

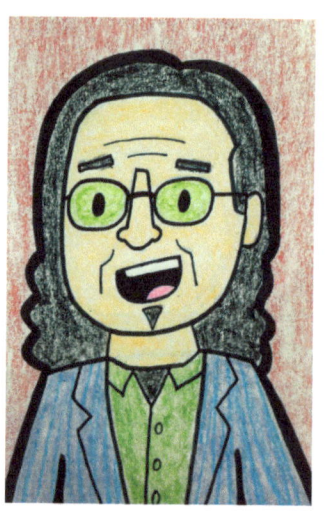

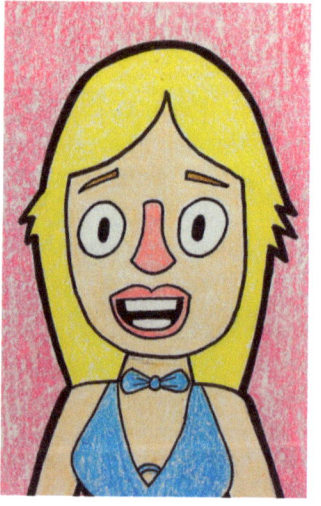

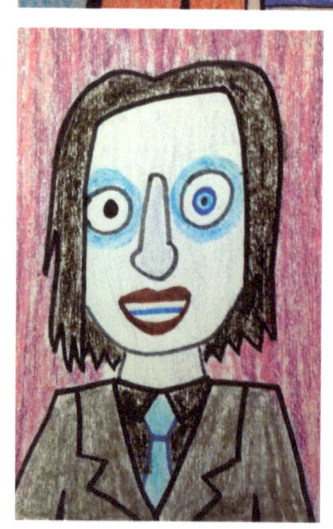

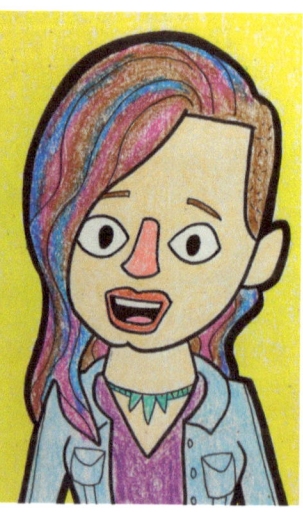

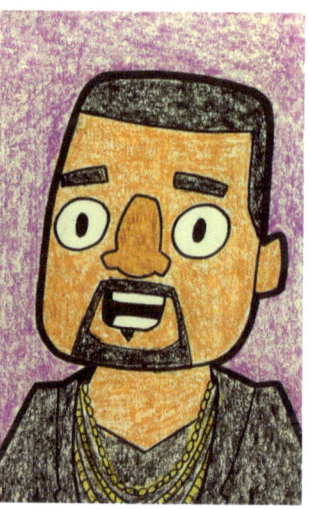

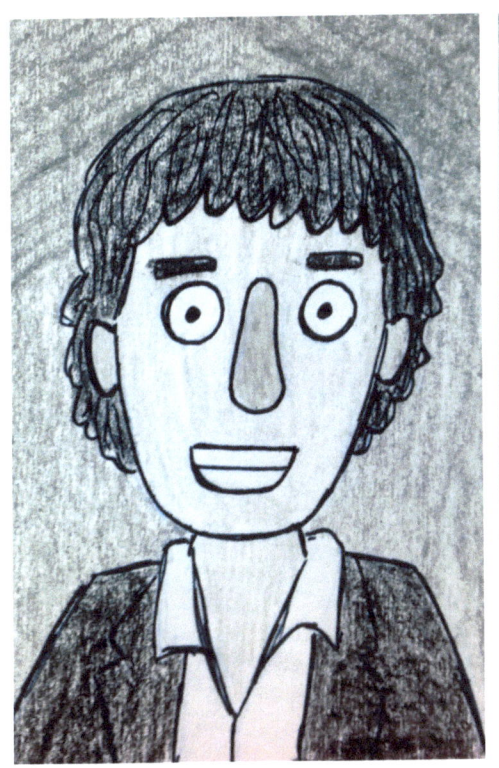

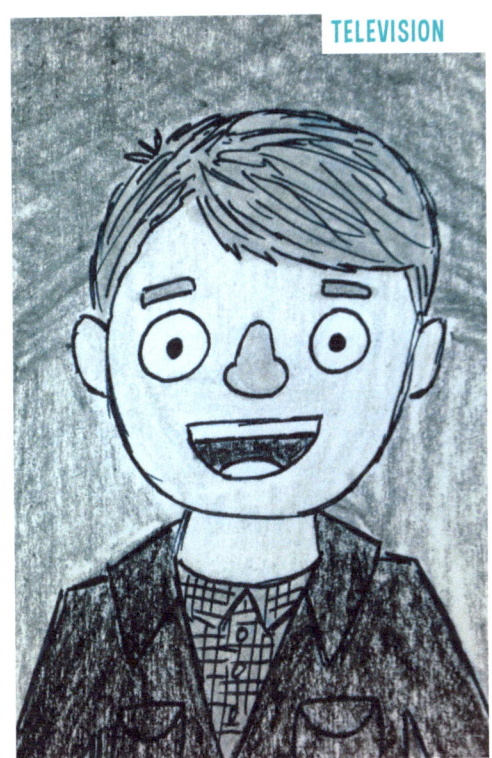

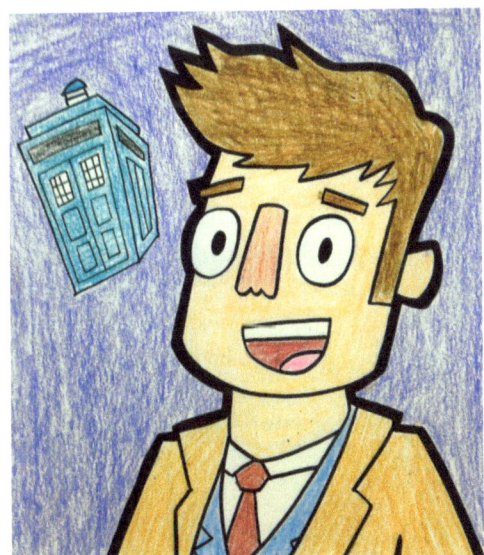

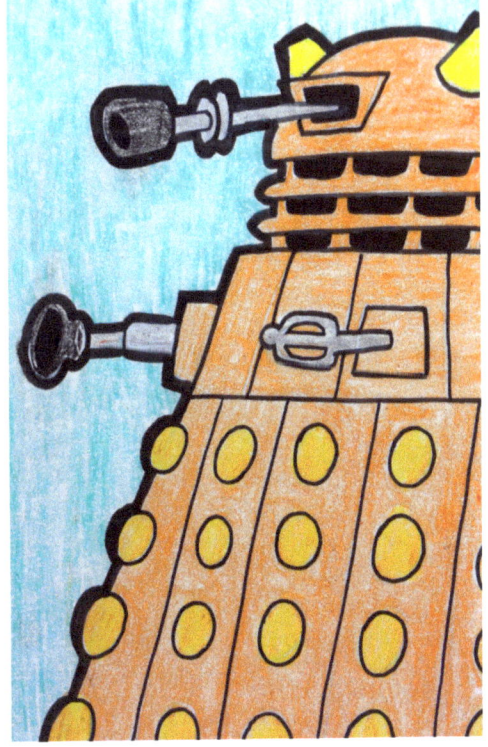

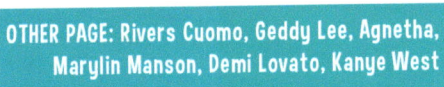

OTHER PAGE: Rivers Cuomo, Geddy Lee, Agnetha, Marylin Manson, Demi Lovato, Kanye West

THIS PAGE: Sherlock Holmes, Watson, Doctor Who, Dalek

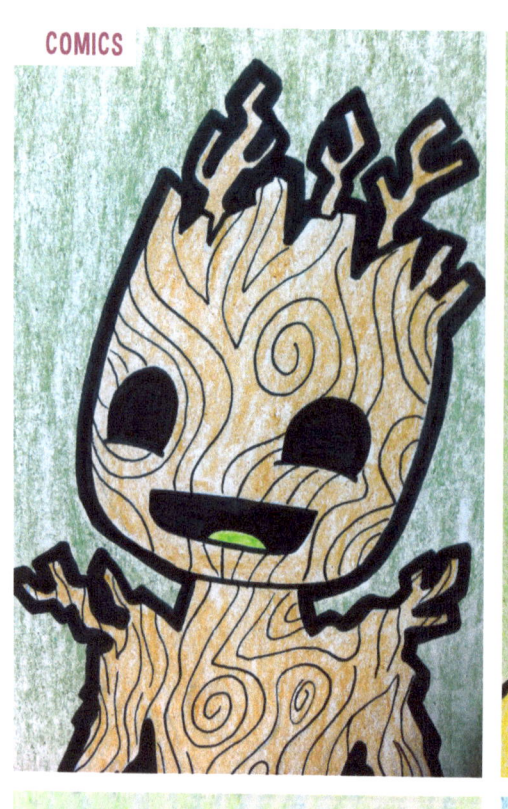
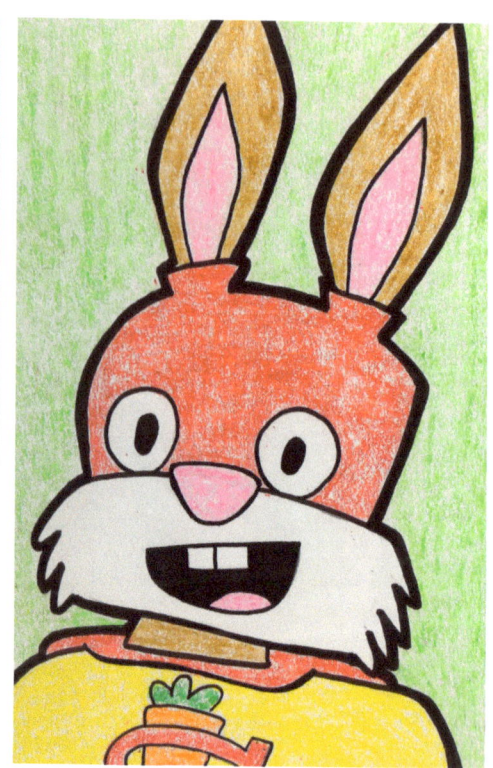
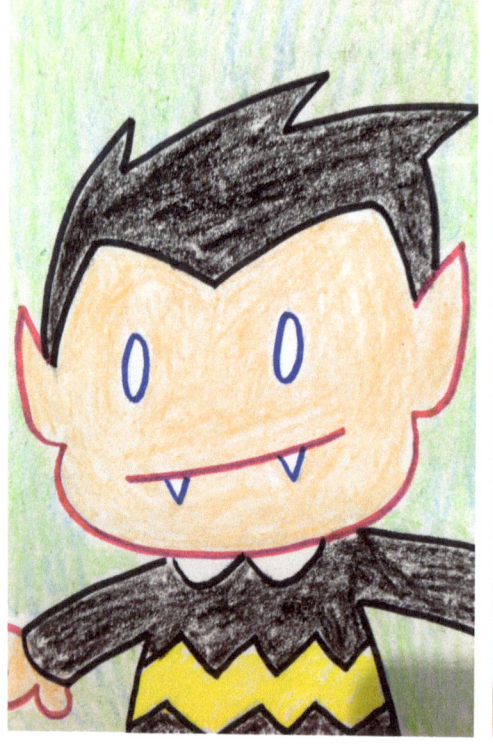
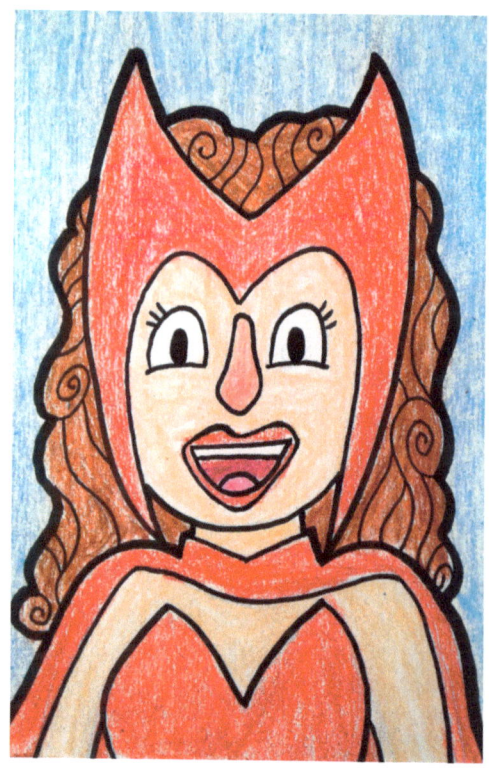

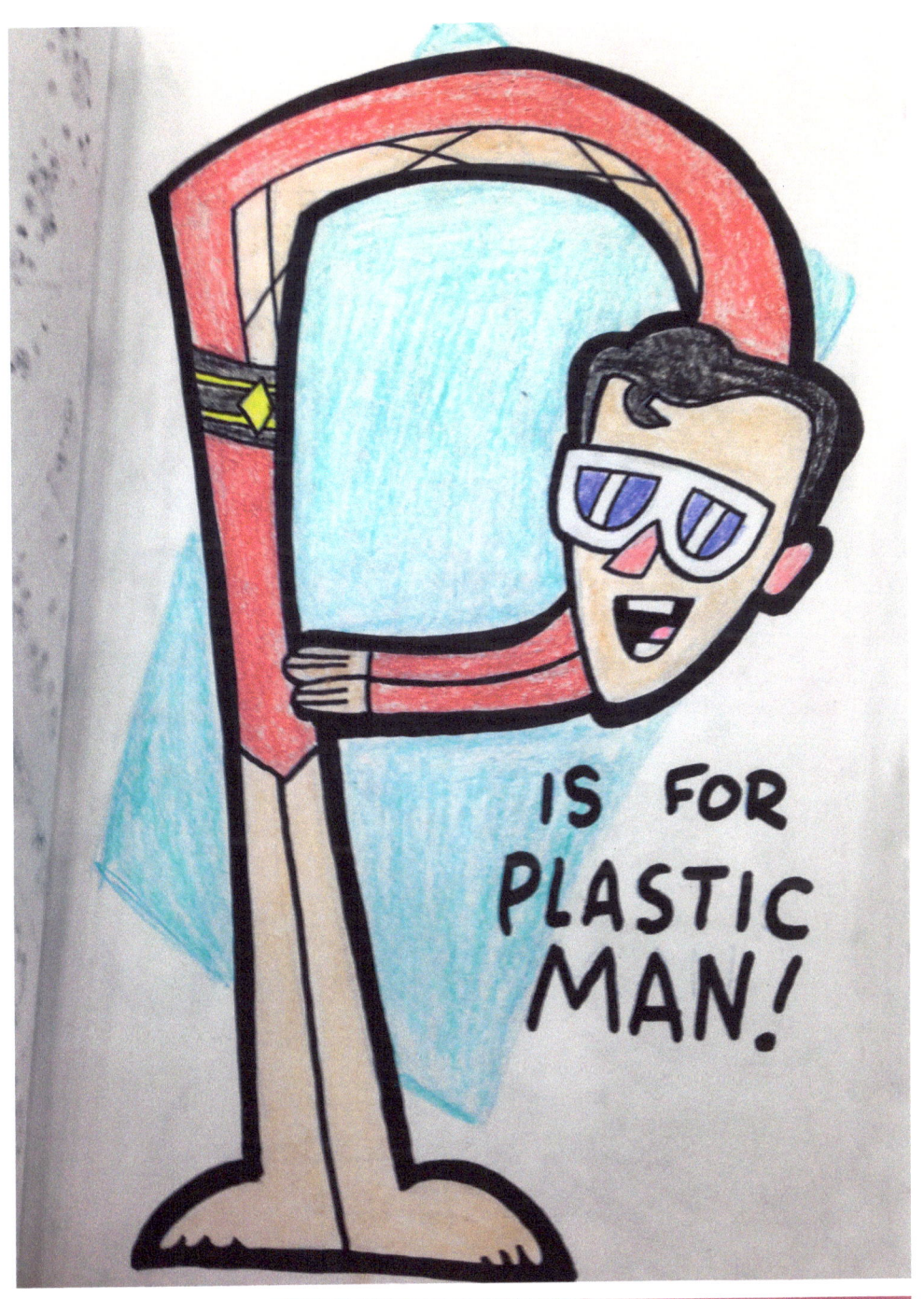

IS FOR PLASTIC MAN!

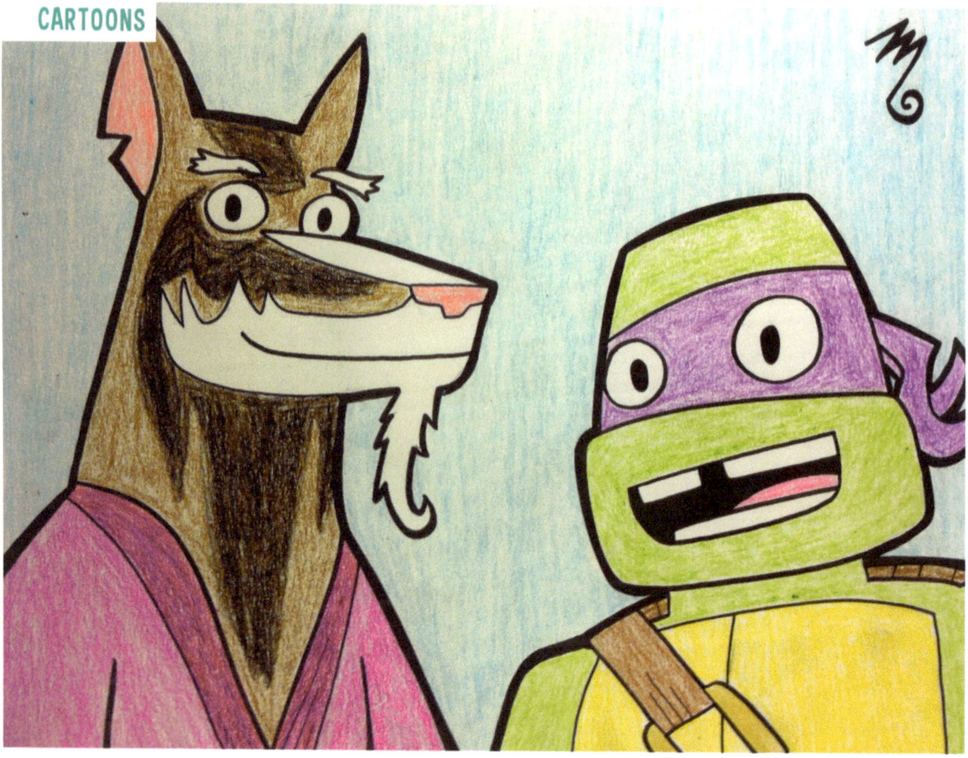

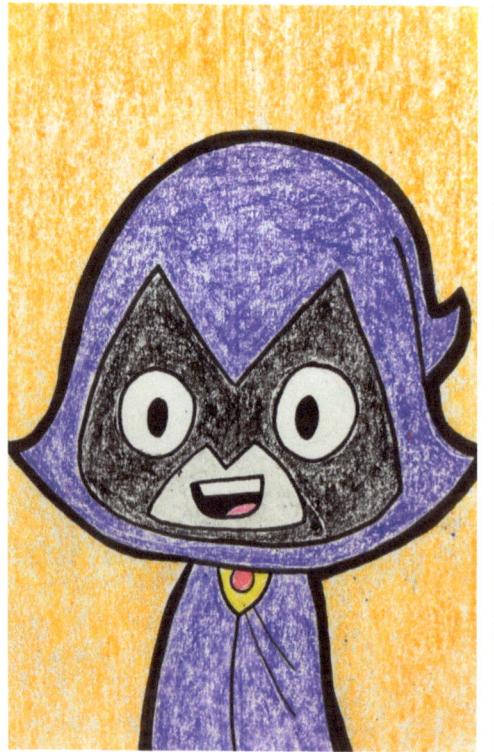

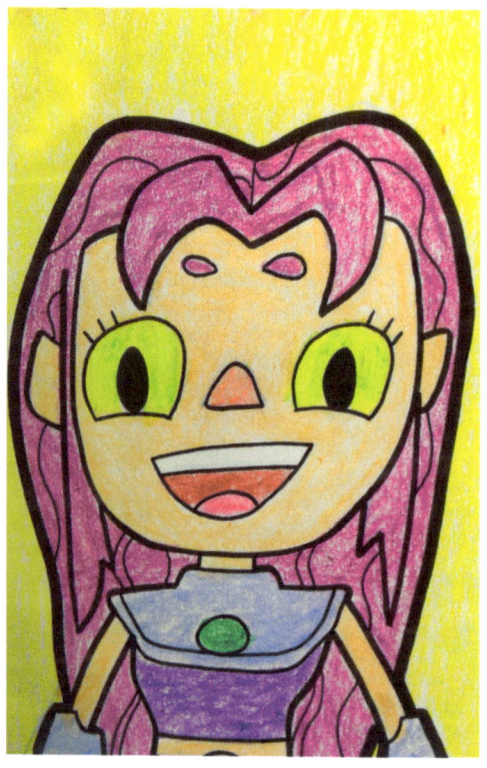

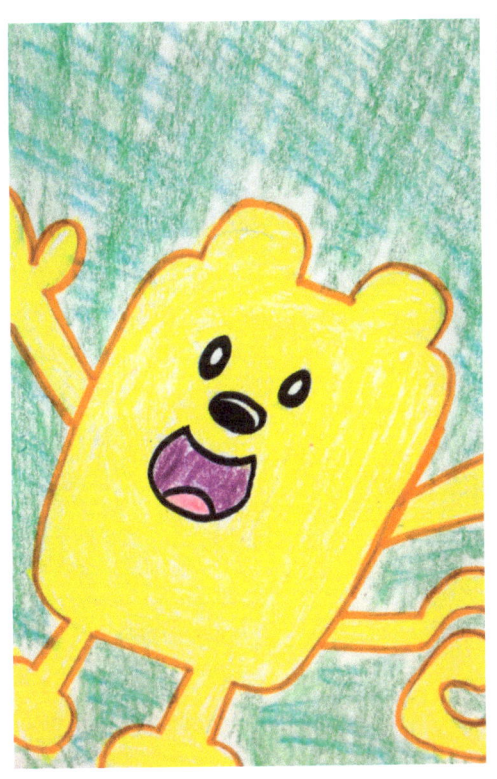

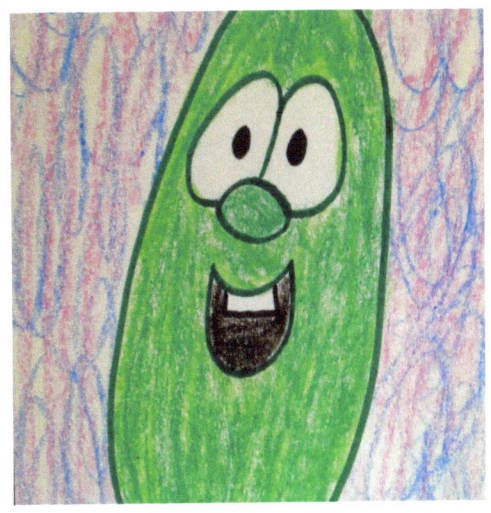

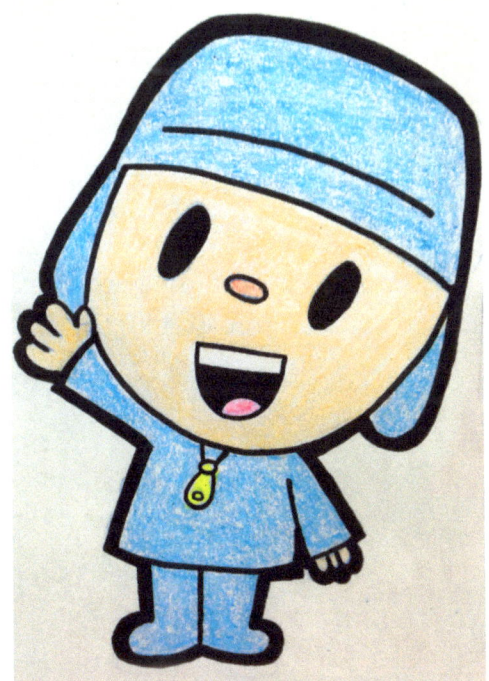

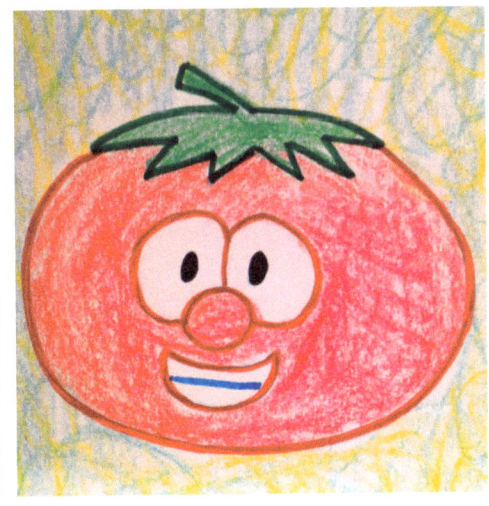

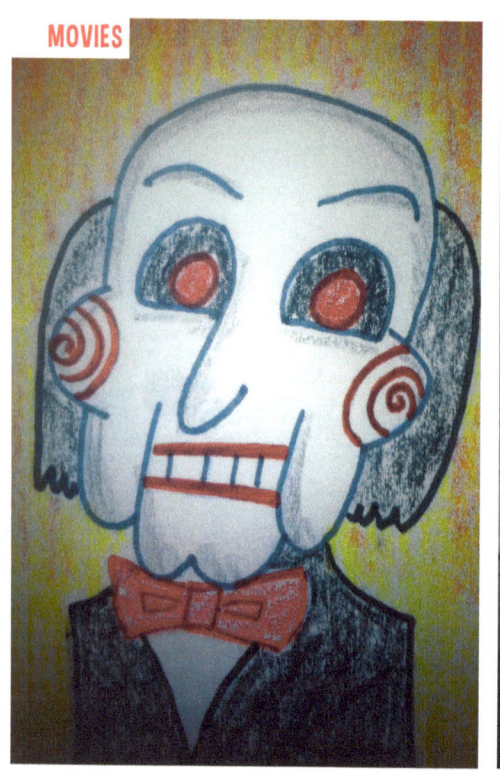
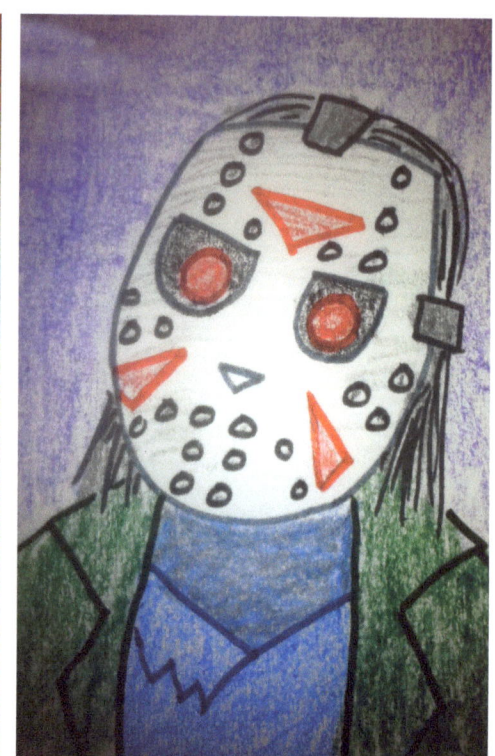
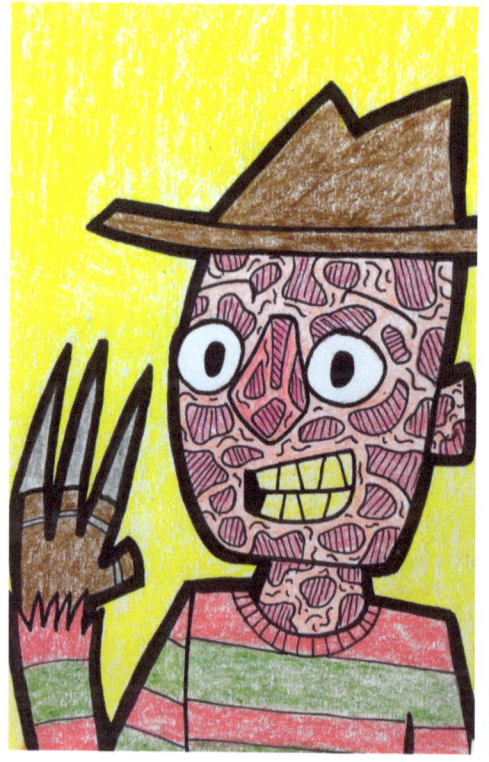
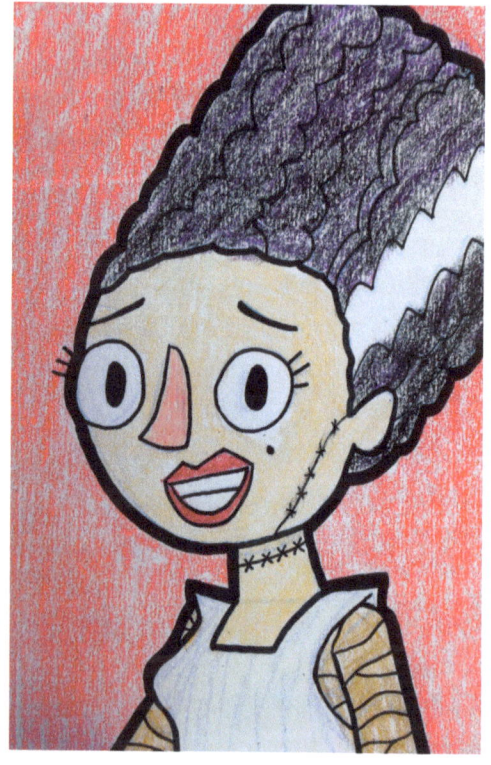

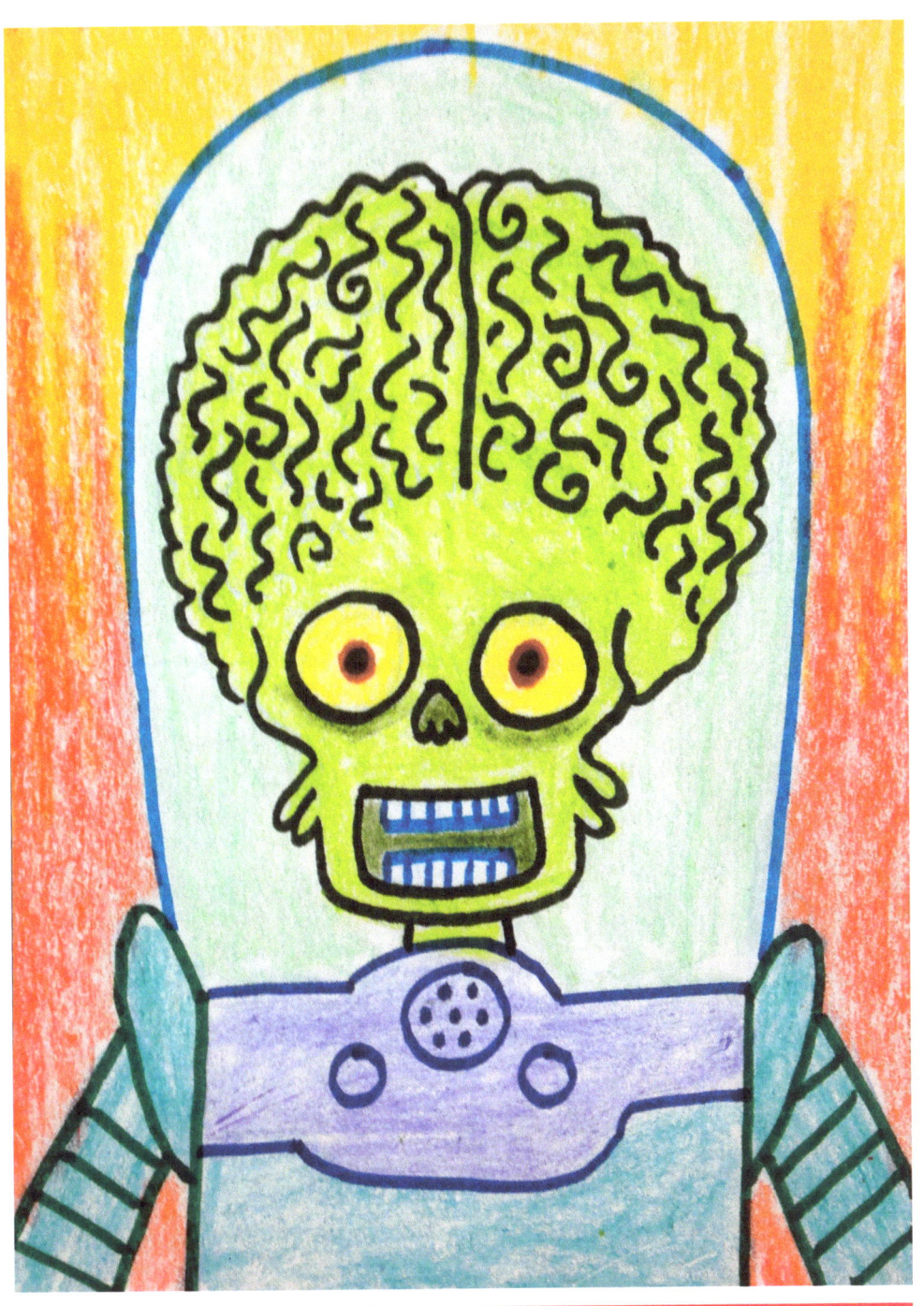

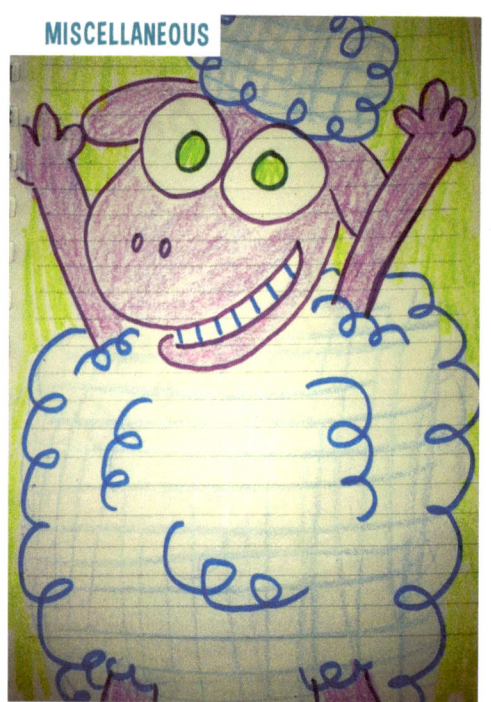

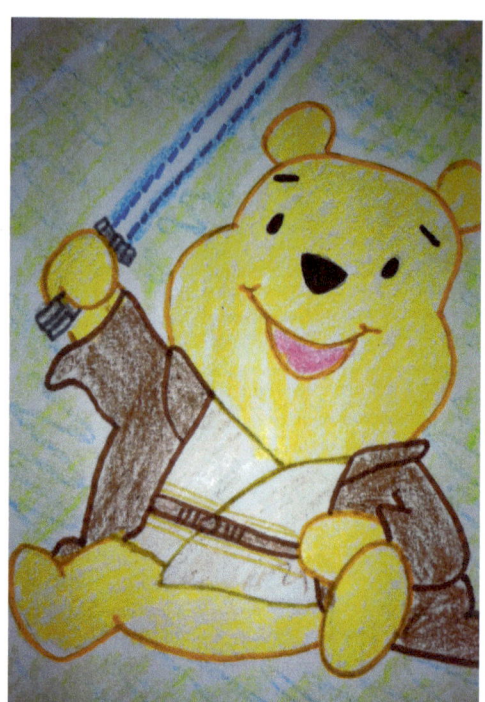

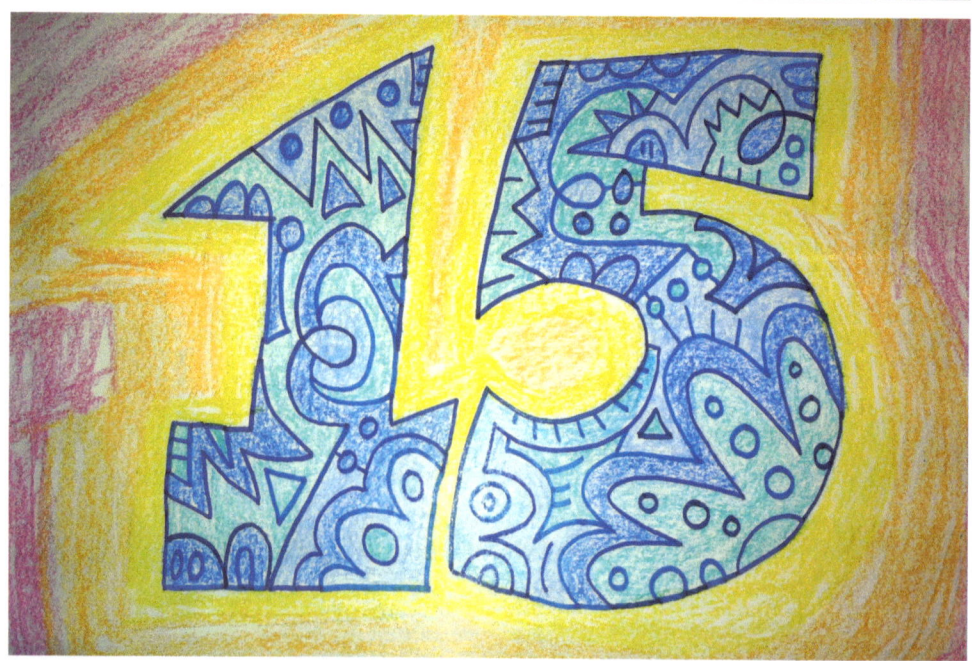

THIS PAGE: Happy Sheep, Jedi Pooh, The Number Fifteen

OTHER PAGE: R2D2 and BMO Dance Off, Marilyn Monroe, Cuddles the Hamster

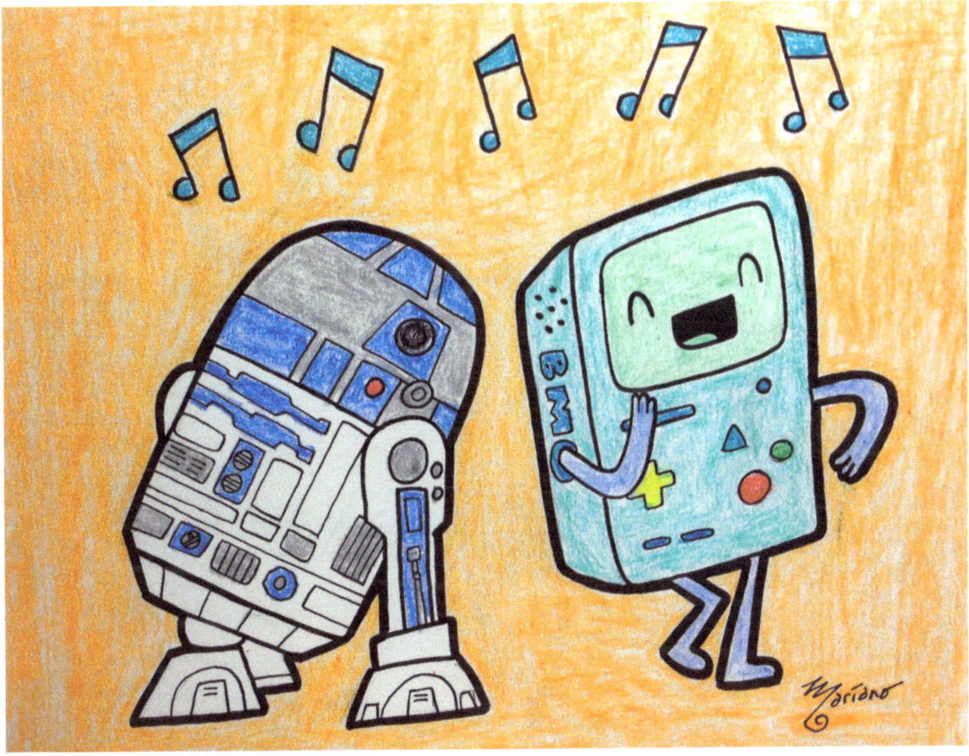

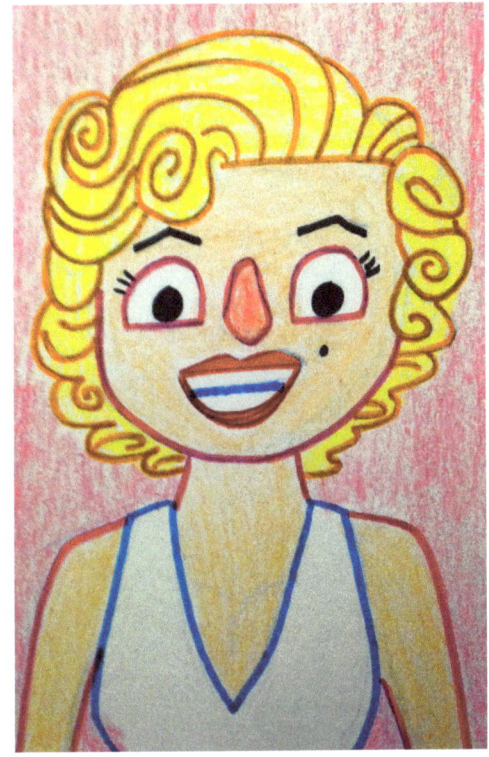
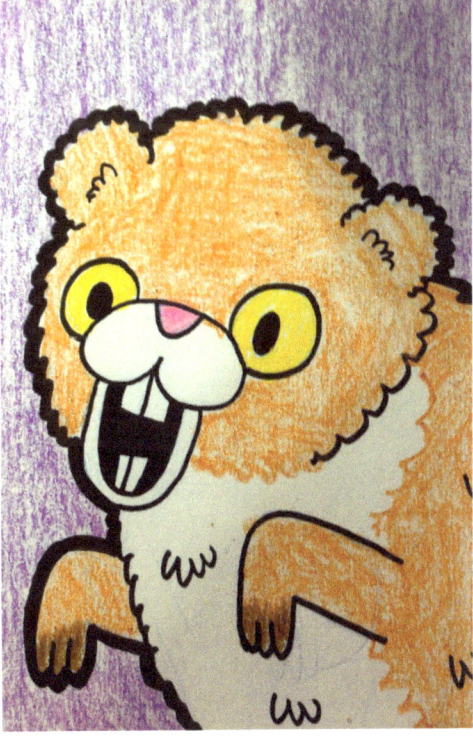

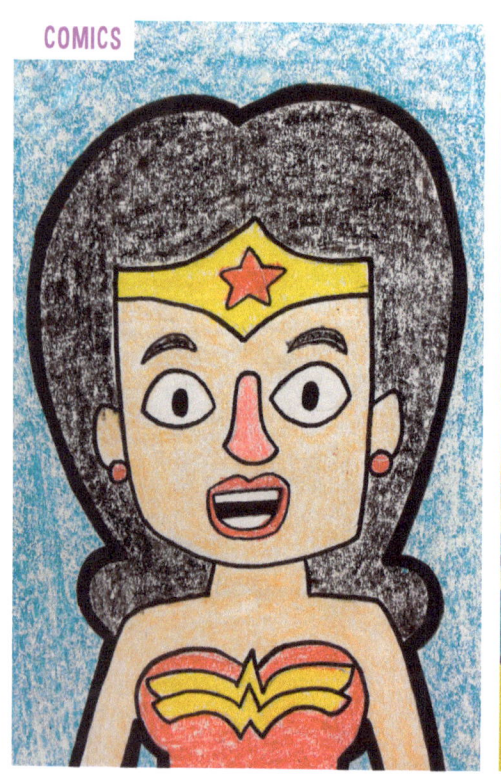

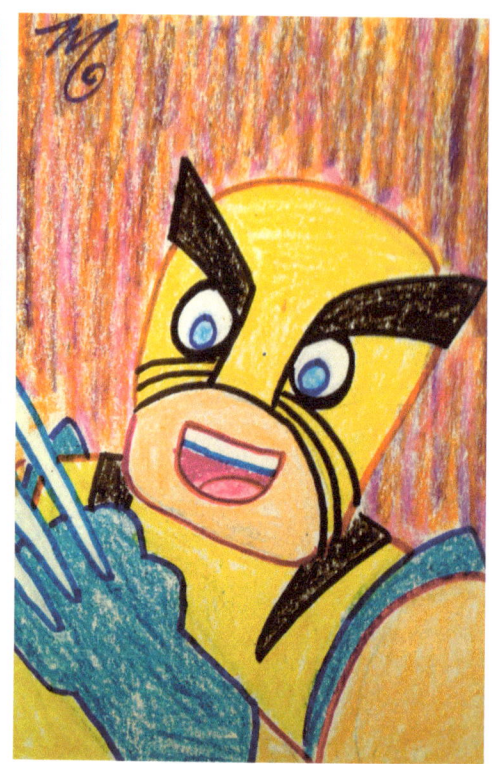

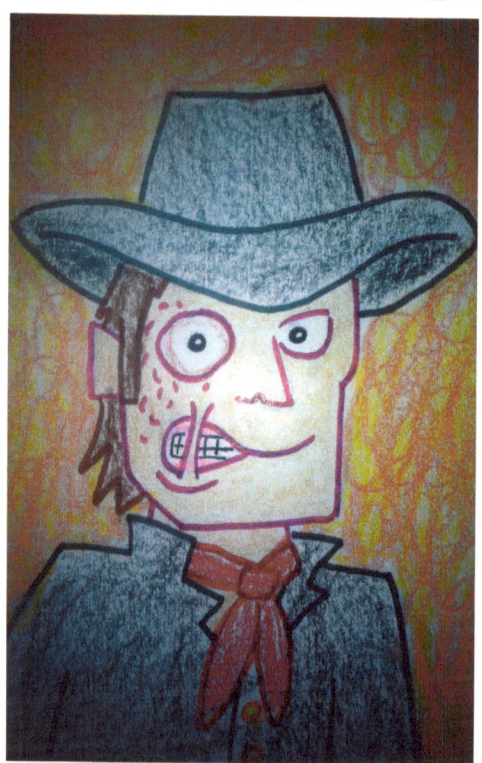

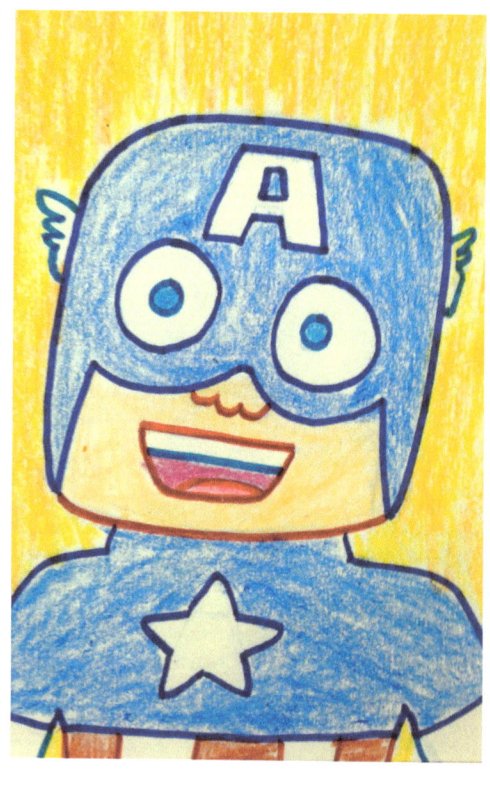

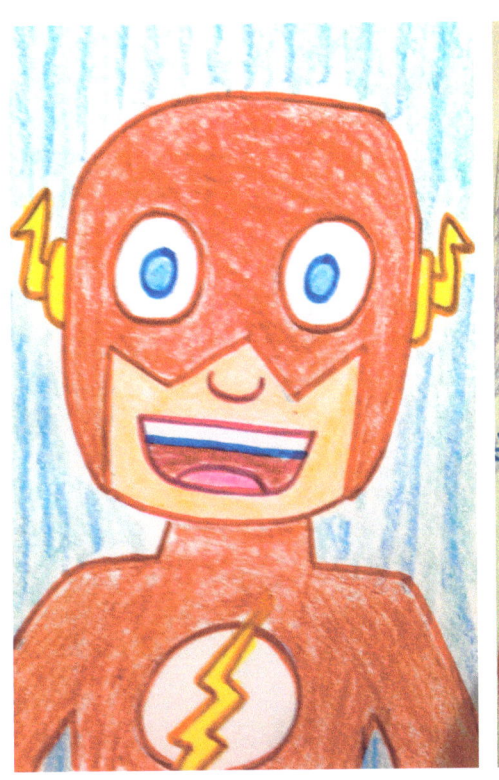
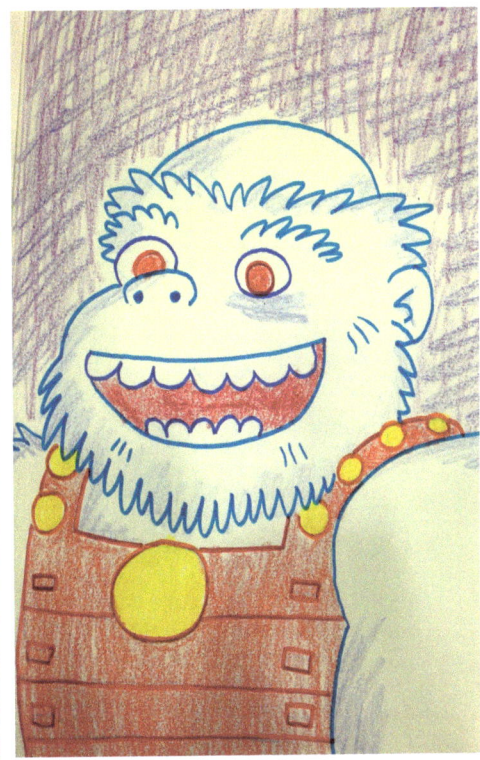
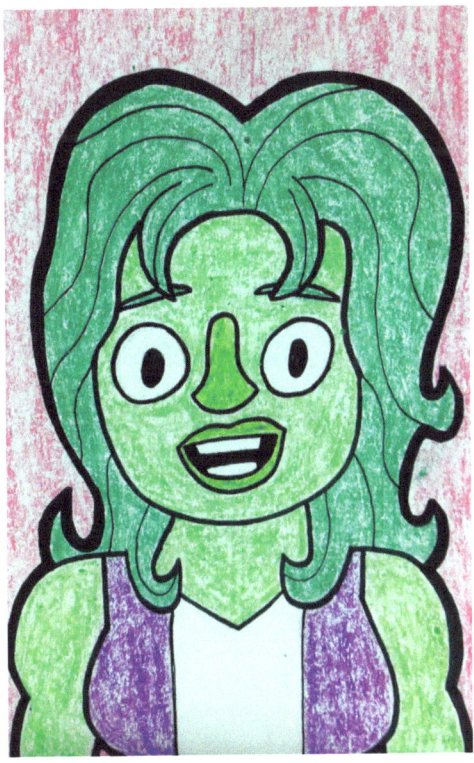
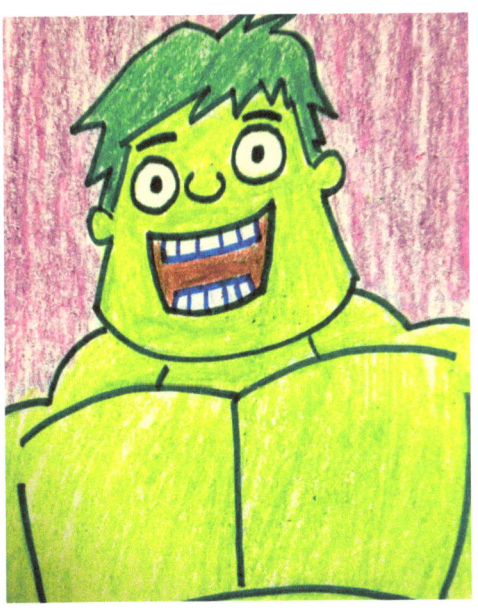

OTHER PAGE: Wonder Woman, Wolverine,
Jonah Hex, Captain America
THIS PAGE: The Flash, Ultra-Humanite,
She-Hulk, Hulk

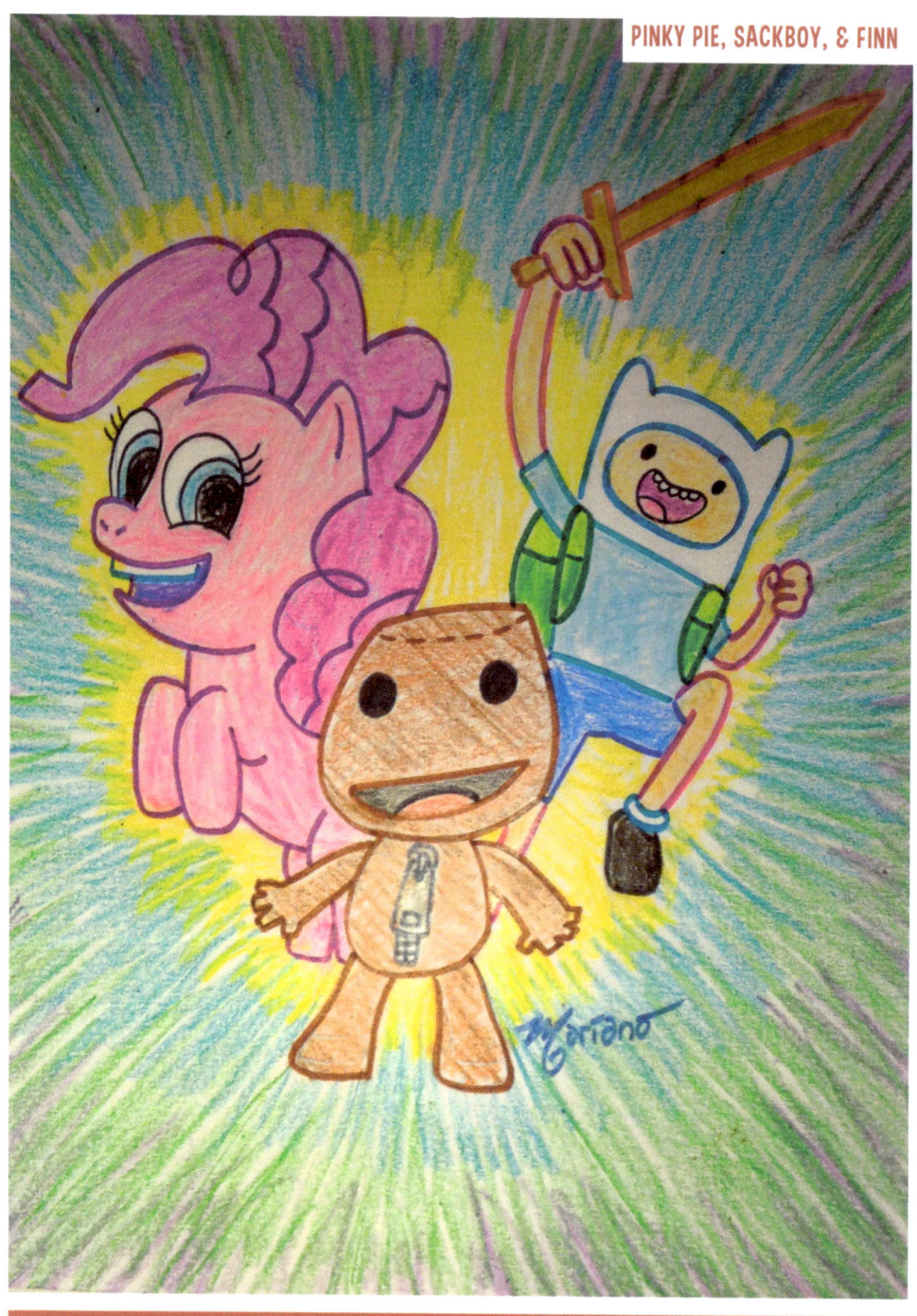

www.ingramcontent.com/pod-product-compliance
Lightning Source LLC
Chambersburg PA
CBHW042023200526
45159CB00035B/3031